THE POLITICS OF CHANGE

The Politics of Change

A Ringside View

N.K. Singh

PENGUIN
VIKING
An imprint of Penguin Random House

VIKING

USA | Canada | UK | Ireland | Australia
New Zealand | India | South Africa | China | Singapore

Viking is part of the Penguin Random House group of companies whose addresses can be found at global.penguinrandomhouse.com

Published by Penguin Random House India Pvt. Ltd
4th Floor, Capital Tower 1, MG Road,
Gurugram 122 002, Haryana, India

First published in Viking by Penguin Books India 2007

10 9 8 7 6 5 4 3 2

Grateful acknowledgements are due to Ambreen Khan and Rakesh Dewal for conceptualizing the book and for marketing support

ISBN 9780670081370

Typeset in Sabon by Mantra Virtual Services, New Delhi
Printed at Replika Press Pvt. Ltd, India

www.penguin.co.in

To

My late parents Tribhuvan and Madhuri

and

Prem Kumari, Meenakshi, Abhijeet, Madhavi

in the belief that politics must change to usher
a prosperous India

Contents

Foreword

N.K. SINGH, or just NK or Nandu to a legion of friends across three generations, can fit many descriptions at the same time. Economist, civil servant, networker, problem-solver, sharp dresser, charmer and so on. Among his numerous talents is the gift of story telling. Of the many stories I remember, two from the early days of the balance of payments crisis under the Narasimha Rao–Manmohan Singh government deserve a mention here. Both of them also feature the other prominent and brilliant reformer of his generation, Montek Singh Ahluwalia.

NK remembers the two of them coming out of the elevator in Paris in 1992 on their way to a meeting with Jacques de Larosière de Chempfeu, then governor of the Bank of France. Montek asked to be excused for a bit to go change because he said he smelled of petrol. In those days, the import of modern-day cleaning equipment was blocked by confiscatory customs duties and so Indian dry cleaners used expensive, polluting petrol that left behind tell-tale fumes. At international venues, it was said that you could sniff the elevator and tell if Indian officials had been in it. Among the first things NK did when he later became revenue secretary was to cut duties on modern-day dry-cleaning machinery.

The second story, which happened in 1993, is set in New York. NK and Montek—then finance secretary—were engaged in high-level negotiations in connection with the aftermath of the balance of payments crisis. They checked into Manhattan's very mid-market UN Park Plaza hotel, a favourite with developing-world officials on tight per diems. The receptionist wouldn't sign them in unless they produced their credit cards and until then, few Indian citizens and certainly not Indian officials, were allowed to use their credit cards overseas. An attaché from the Indian consulate saved them the blushes by covering for them with his card. Next morning, a telephone call was made to S. Venkitaramanan, then governor of RBI, to allow frequent overseas travellers, including officials, to use their credit cards.

NK can tell you a thousand such stories but these two stand out because they show quickness of thinking, resourcefulness and an instinctively reformist mindset. They also underline the distance we have travelled on the reform path and the degree of difficulty faced by the pioneers who started out in our pseudo-socialist times.

I will not waste time talking about NK's charm, hospitality and networking skills because these are already legendary and I will not praise his truly remarkable sartorial taste because I am the one person least qualified to talk about sharp dressing. But I will say this about him. Whenever there is a really complicated problem to be solved, or one that involves politics, bureaucracy and corporates working at cross purposes and with conflicting interests, it would help if NK was somewhere in that loop.

His most remarkable talent, a real gift, is problem-solving, of getting things done. Is it any wonder then, in the still very early days of reform, ICICI was transformed into a fully private bank, without protest or noise? Today, fifteen years after reforms began, you cannot sell 5 per cent in Neyveli Lignite.

This selection of NK's very fine, very popular and very informative columns from the *Indian Express* and the *Financial Express* on subjects ranging from the initiation of reforms in infrastructure, the insurance sector, centre–state relations, coalition politics, global perspectives on India and challenges the country continues to face on the reform path, will be essential reading for any student of the history of Indian economic reforms.

I hope the publication of *The Politics of Change* will encourage NK to write his memoirs; that is what we all await. The problem with memoirs, however, is that you write them only when you retire. And NK, true to the words of his most recent boss, Atal Bihari Vajpayee, is not the kind to either tire or retire in a hurry. And surely, none of his friends would ever wish him to.

28 May 2007
New Delhi

Shekhar Gupta

Preface

The essays contained in this book are commentaries on some of our more significant economic challenges. While being snapshots in time they also have a more abiding relevance on the policy changes needed to sustain the current growth momentum.

On a flight back from San Francisco to London on 6 June 2004 after the Fifth Annual Stanford India Economic Conference, Shekhar Gupta, Editor-in-Chief, *Indian Express*, enquired whether I had any firm assignments after retirement from government service. I did mention some quasi-academic work and plans to continue my engagement with several research organizations. Shekhar however suggested that it would be to everybody's benefit if I wrote a regular column for the *Indian Express*.

On my return to Delhi, I called on P. Chidambaram and mentioned Shekhar's proposal. He greatly encouraged me to accept the offer and was confident that the discipline of writing columns could be a new way to discover myself. Chidambaram himself had been a popular columnist when out of office and wrote the column 'Politically Correct'. By the time I received the formal offer from the *Indian Express*, I had already made up my mind to accept. Suhel Seth helped me to firm up the caption 'From the Ringside' which is now the subtitle of this book.

I must record my special appreciation to Jessica S. Wallack, Assistant Professor at the University of California, San Diego for her continuous support and, in fact, several columns appearing in the book have been jointly authored by us.

My thanks are also due to research assistants, Vaibhav Gupta,

Sridhar Kundu and Siba Prasad Tripathy for statistical data and analytical support. S.R. Raja, assisted by S. Gopalakrishnan has given me excellent secretarial support throughout.

These essays would not have been possible without the valuable support of the Observer Research Foundation to whom I remain deeply indebted.

I have thoroughly enjoyed this new endeavour; by the time this book comes out I will have written nearly 125 essays. This book captures the crux of many of these articles although it is less than half of what I have written.

Its outcome is now for the readers to evaluate.

17 May 2007 **N.K. Singh**
New Delhi

Introduction

India has never been quick to change. We gained independence with lofty ideals and high aspirations and spent the next few decades growing at 3 per cent annually. We conquered our worries about food security, but we then never moved to the next generation of productive agri-business and agro-processing. The agricultural sector is still a reform priority.

We built up an elaborate state apparatus to aid in economic planning, industrialization and investment—that was in many ways the conventional wisdom about development in those days—but we did not dismantle it when conventional wisdom changed. Instead, we saw a gradual accretion of the state during the 1970s.

The 1980s brought tentative reforms and the 1990s, some more. The balance of payments crisis in 1991 (to some extent brought about as a side-effect of halting reform and the fiscal choices of the 1980s) did force us somewhat to jolt forward on the path to reforms. We reduced tariff barriers, removed industrial licensing, opened most sectors to foreign investment and embarked on a still-unfolding quest towards public–private partnerships in infrastructure and social services. Our rhetoric evolved: new initiatives are now increasingly referred to as 'business plans'.

Sometimes we've reached this point in convoluted ways. For example, take the case of India's telecom sector: deregulation and corporatization of the state-owned telecom service provider has been one of the major changes over the past decade.

How did it happen? It happened as part of a deal to award telecom employees a generous package of benefits. The then communications minister, Ram Vilas Paswan, had carried his record of announcing populist schemes in railways over to telecom and announced a substantial phone largesse to all telecom employees on 12 June 2000. The package, in which each of the 3.2 lakh employees of the department of telecom services would be given a telephone connection free with 250 free calls a month and a waiver of Rs 150 off the monthly rental, would have cost the exchequer at least Rs 300 crore a year. The move was widely criticized, particularly by the finance ministry, and there was pressure on Paswan to roll back this decision. A revised version of the benefit was ultimately accepted (in a meeting held at the residence of Prime Minister Vajpayee where I was also present), but simultaneously, the date of 31 October 2000 was also announced for the corporatization of the telecom services in the form of Bharat Sanchar Nigam Ltd.

The results speak for themselves. The economic policy changes of the past decade and a half have unleashed a side of India that has taken the world by storm. We are now one of the world's emerging growth centres, a high-profile contributor to software and IT innovation, the back office to the world and, more recently, 'Incredible India'. Economic growth has accelerated to 8 per cent; almost triple the average during the 1960s and 1970s.

Just to illustrate the changes: in 1991, Montek Ahluwalia and I waited outside the office of David Mulford seeking accommodation on harsh conditionalities being imposed by the IMF. We were in a similar position later with the US treasury, reiterating this request with Lawrence Summers. Not so many years later, Mulford came to see me, both in the finance ministry and in the prime minister's office. Larry Summers frequently lectures in India on its many notable successes (as well as our need to address many remaining challenges).

More generally, investors' perceptions of India's new role started with cautious optimism, swelled to enthusiasm after India's high rates of growth in 2005–06, and are now generally positive though not ebullient. Some of the early essays in the book document the last few years of the world's views on India as I have experienced them in my travels, participating in global economic summits such as those held in Davos or Aspen and in my work on various commissions.

But we have a long way to go. It is not clear how long the

opportunity and favourable external views of India will last, or how sustainable the current growth trends are without further reforms by the centre and state governments. Not only do states' decisions affect the nation's overall fiscal balance (as illustrated in 'The Economically Illiterate Populism of Manifestos'), they are also important partners in economic reforms.

The worries on everyone's minds have also evolved. Debt and debt crises—inherently a zero-sum game—are still concerns, and there is even more uncertainty about the trajectory of global financial and demographic imbalances as discussed in 'A New Year beyond Resolutions'. Concerns about energy security and global warming have risen on the priority list. India's domestic energy policies, especially pricing, affect the prospects for international environmental sustainability as much as environmental concerns affect our own growth prospects. 'The Energy Paradigm: Back to the Future' discusses some of the risks, while 'Energy Prices Vs Global Warming' shows the importance of India's domestic politics for international outcomes.

The new 'flat world' (to use Thomas Friedman's memorable phrase) has also exposed some fault lines in the international context that India will have to respond to. Shifting demographics and patterns of economic activity, not to mention greater global awareness of the opportunities to be had in other countries have increased migration pressures. 'Multiple Challenges of Global Migration' and 'Brain Gain Vs Brain Drain', based on some of my work in the United Nations Global Commission on Migration, describe the magnitude of the migration flows and the issues involved. International migration continues to be limited and distorted by a patchwork of national laws. Their effect on both the country of origin and destination countries have attracted increasing political and policy attention, but ineffective international action.

Second, economic cooperation and competition co-exist uneasily in this era of shifting economic centres of gravity. The essays on India and China bring out the different perspectives on one of the most significant relationships: on the one hand, we ask who will win the race; on the other hand, we have a lot to gain by collaborating.

These tensions and uncertainties are sure to continue as the global economy evolves. 'Do Nations Have the Collective Guts to Look

Global Risk in the Face?' provides an overview of some of the challenges that international institutions face. The essays on the global context, however, contain more questions than answers; questions that India must continue to ask and evaluate as the context and the opportunities change.

Many would say that we are at an inflexion point; that we are gathering momentum that cannot be stopped—even by the remaining state apparatus. India is a future economic superpower, that poverty will be halved in the next decade. The diversity of policies and outcomes among India's states provides some hints that this trajectory is not automatic.

Even as the international economic context has changed to favour countries like India, India itself must prepare to compete. We need to reinvigorate and restructure our economic diplomacy. In some cases, this means building stronger governmental and non-governmental relationships with countries—through trade agreements (as explained in 'Preferential Trade Agreements: Stumbling Blocks or Building Blocks'), student exchanges, strategic dialogues, even participation in sports or building the infrastructure to encourage tourism. 'Tenets of Economic Diplomacy' gives a view of the range of ways to engage the international economy, while 'Taking the French Connection beyond Wine and Cheese' applies these principles. Economic diplomacy, however, involves domestic change as much as anything else.

We also need to look at our domestic concerns. There are signs that the current growth trends are simply the slack being taken from the system: entrepreneurial drive, pent up for decades, taking advantage of the stock of skilled labour and underdeveloped market. We are already seeing bottlenecks that have only gotten worse as economic activity has accelerated: infrastructure is one, skilled labour is another. We are also running up against environmental limits like air pollution and water shortages.

The need for domestic reforms to take advantage of international economic opportunities is nowhere more apparent than in our business climate and its competitiveness with other countries. To paraphrase Larry Summers's March 2006 address to CII on India's rising prominence and remaining policy obstacles, 'We must fear the lack of fear'.

'The Quest for "Pahale India"' and 'What Gets Measured Gets Done' are just two of the many essays I've written on India's business climate in international comparison and its impact on the discussions of India in various international settings.

India's prospects as a 'knowledge economy' are also mixed if immediate attention is not given to the educational system and to legal support for intellectual property rights. At one level, protecting intellectual property seems simple: it is the 'product' of the new economy. On the other hand, 'knowledge' is harder to segment than automobiles, toys, cloth, or other manufactured goods where 'property' is reasonably protected. 'Patents Act: Not a Magic Bullet but a Necessary Pill' and 'The Battle for Knowledge Economy' look at some of these issues.

Order in the fiscal house also needs to be addressed. Fiscal policies too come up in many essays in some way, but 'Getting Cross with Cross-Subsidies' and 'Time to Repeal Small Cess Acts' lay out some of the specific changes to our fiscal policies that would be steps towards fiscal prudence.

The real foundation of the fiscal house, however, lies in the federal arrangements and the incentives that these create for central and state budgeting. The 'fiscal house' is actually more like a 'fiscal compound' in India—a collection of government budgets with expenditure plans and revenue efforts influenced by each other's actions. I raise several suggestions for reforms in the essays: the most applicable on this point is that we must develop a clearer, more unified mechanism for allocating funds. The Planning Commission and the Finance Commission operate independently, sometimes asynchronously, to determine transfers that cannot be thought of separately without losing coherence in fiscal planning.

Public expenditure management is also at least as important as fiscal policy per se to ensure that India's public resources are used to maximum advantage. 'The Eleventh Plan, or the Eleventh Version of the Same Plan?'and 'Put the Finance Ministry on the Reforms Path' step back to critique the larger context of public expenditure decision making. 'Bridging the Gap between Outlays and Outcomes' and 'Getting Projects on Track' take a more micro-level approach to analysing project management and accountability. Again, states have an important role to play in connecting allocations to outcomes. Many of the central government funds set aside for particular state programs go unspent—not because states don't need the rural roads, the rural electrification or other benefits, but because states can't spend the funds. States and local governments are also in the best position to identify needs and prioritize expenditures, but few have the necessary personnel and administrative structures.

These kinds of reforms of the public expenditure framework fall short of reexamining the public sector in development. Disinvestment, a.k.a. privatization, has been one of the so-called third rails of politics over the decade, now as much as ever. Several essays in the book deal with the consequences of the inaction, especially in infrastructure. Given that electricity, transport and telecommunications function as systems, the quality of the system is only as good as the weakest link.

No one priority has as many essays devoted to it as infrastructure. Seven essays examine various aspects of the infrastructure dilemma. These essays span topics such as public sector infrastructure behemoths (When Sacred Cows Block the Intersection), civil aviation ('Fear of Flying'), finance ('Foreign Exchange Reserves Are No Magic Wand') and telecom ('Telecom Tales: The Choice before India'). The continued relevance of many of the recommendations is disappointing.

As mentioned previously, telecom has been perhaps the most successful area of infrastructure reform in terms of both procedures and outcomes. We have created a relatively independent regulator (not the first time around, but the second), and we have attracted substantial private investment. Public operators' performance has improved dramatically, whether one measures it in terms of the faster installation of fixed lines, more competitive pricing, or closer focus on consumer preferences. But even here, we still have not lived up to our potential. Rural tele-density remains low by any standards and congestion of the network (especially at points of interchange with the public sector providers) remains a concern. The spectrum allocation debate—a difficult one on mainly technical grounds, never mind the politics and varying interests—has gone on for too long.

Transport reforms have hit a similar roadblock, so to speak. On the one hand, there are some triumphs. The national highway system has created functional links between major economic centres, and the National Highways Authority has, for the most part, been a strong foundation for public–private partnerships. The use of the fuel cess as collateral for finance has worked well. The civil aviation landscape has been transformed—more airlines, more flights, lower prices, more people flying than ever before—since it was opened to private competition in 1994. Ports have inched towards smoother handling of cargo and some private terminals have come up.

Railways, on the other hand, remains steadfastly resistant to much change. It has improved its financial performance recently, but it is hard to say whether this is a sustainable shift or one based on short-term cost-cutting without regard to longer-term maintenance of capital.

Many of our transport hubs are becoming increasingly congested under pressure as other parts of the network liberalize and traffic increases. Inland container depots, for example, impose a cap on goods movement through ports, no matter how much any particular port improves. Paucity of runway space at airports and air traffic controller staff strength create similar obstacles for flights. Urban traffic congestion has become mind-boggling: flyovers cannot keep up with the increasing number of vehicles and comprehensive rethinking of urban transport is impossible given the difficulties of land acquisition.

But electricity stands out as the infrastructure sector in which reform policies and reform realities have the biggest disconnect. Several essays discuss various aspects of the policy changes—the Electricity Act of 2003, the mega power projects, the Integrated Energy Policy and others—and the absence of actual changes. The electricity sector's future is essentially in the hands of state governments—these are the authorities that determine the prospects for independent regulation, reform of the distribution sector, reshaping and re-invigorating of a substantial portion of the generation and transmission assets in the network, as well as implementing decisions for new generation capacity.

In the end, achieving all of these policy goals comes down to the politics of change. Every one of the essays in this book contains some hint of politics. This is inevitable—my years in organizations ranging from the Bihar State Electricity Board to the finance ministry to the

Union Planning Commission and the Prime Minister's Office and, most recently, the Bihar State Planning Commission have exposed me to the full range of the politics of policies.

My early years of service in Bihar gave me first-hand experience with the struggles of an over-regulated, underdeveloped state grappling to improve power availability, repair its finances and carry out rural developmental programmes efficiently.

State administrations continue to be, in many ways, the 'front line' of India's development policies. Many of the schemes conceived at the centre end up being implemented at this level. Many of the problems for which there is no scheme end up with policy-makers at this level. And ultimately the citizens and voters expect as much (if not more) from their state representatives. We need to take a closer look at how these can be made more effective.

When I moved from Bihar to the central government, the initial stint in the ministry of commerce put me in a position to observe the making of a more internationally-oriented policy: the trade regime. At the time this was controlled, with quantitative restrictions and high tariffs. It was a struggle to secure limited market access through bilateral barter trade agreements with Russia and the east European economies.

My next five years in Tokyo from 1981–85 came at a time when tentative reforms had begun. I gained experience in international trade diplomacy: my successful negotiations with Suzuki enabled the opening of the automobile market, an important growth driver.

This experience proved useful much later in my career when it—being the point man in the ministry of finance to negotiate the agreements with the International Monetary Fund (IMF) and the World Bank between 1991 and 1993—gave me a first-hand feel of negotiations with multilateral institutions. This is always an attempt to balance the pace of change with retention of social cohesiveness. In some ways, the same negotiation skills have proved useful in working in the domestic arena as well.

The subsequent years as expenditure secretary and revenue secretary were spent in budget-making, improving expenditure management systems and shaping tax policy reforms—all of which gives me a window into what is happening in the ring now.

My time 'in the ring' took me through many other policy areas over the 1990s. As secretary to the prime minister, member of the Planning Commission, and head of various task forces on telecom, foreign investment, power, textiles and energy reforms, I was part of the wider deregulation that has taken place since the balance of payments crisis.

The years in the Planning Commission were also an education in the dynamics of centre–state relations; the diversity in governance quality and the need to improve the consultative mechanisms in a new context.

My years of interacting with multilateral institutions and bodies like the Global Environment Facility, WIPO Advisory Group on Privatization and the UN Global Commission on International Migration have also informed my views from the ringside. Participation in global summits in Davos, ASPEN and Interactive India specific sessions at INSEAD, Wharton as well as annual conferences at Stanford, a blend of academics with policy makers, taught me the complexities in implementing technocratic advice in an era of uncertain coalition politics.

One lesson has been clear: consensus is harder to maintain than controversy, whether among politicians or within society. Half the book is about the politics of change in all its glory, so I will include just a few telling incidents to illustrate the kinds of politics we have to change.

Financial sector reforms have long been on the anvil and have been inching along in some ways and not as much in others. Finance Minister Yashwant Sinha introduced a bill in parliament to amend the Bank Nationalization Act by diluting the government equity to 33 per cent in all nationalized banks except the State Bank of India. While he did (cosmetically) argue that the 'public sector character' of the bank would be retained, this would have unleashed competitiveness in the banking sector and reduced the cost of financial intermediation.

I, among others, was asked to solicit the cooperation of other political parties when there was a prolonged stalemate in the standing committee of parliament to which the bill was referred. When I met Manmohan Singh, at that time the leader of the opposition in the Rajya Sabha, he was candid enough to explain that there was no consensus in the Congress Party on this proposal and, irrespective of his personal views, bank nationalization was a touchy subject 'since many remained nostalgic about Mrs Indira Gandhi having nationalized the banks in 1969'. The bill lapsed and no one, of course, expects the present UPA government to revive it in any form.

That was a classic case of diverging philosophies, but sometimes the politics of no change is just that: politics. Foreign investment in the insurance sector was always a contentious issue. The IRDA Bill 1999 opened the sector a little, but the Lok Sabha debate suggests that apart from restricting the limit of foreign equity in the insurance sector to 26 per cent and agreeing that any change on this limit would necessitate a legislative amendment were part of dynamics of negotiation with senior Congress leaders. While submitting the report on foreign investment in 2003, I had proposed raising this cap from 26 per cent to 49 per cent but any serious consideration of the proposal was postponed in the short period which was left before the sudden announcement of general elections.

It is ironic that this very change was proposed by Chidambaram two years ago in his Budget speech, but this time around the other coalition partners of the UPA government are opposed to the change. The proposal lies in limbo. So while it was initially the Congress which insisted on a legislative limit of 26 per cent, just a few years later they themselves find it difficult to implement the very change which had earlier been opposed. We must change the politics, at centre, state, and centre–state levels.

States have always had many constitutionally guaranteed policy prerogatives, but these have been de facto constrained by the central government's fiscal dominance and the internal dynamics of all-encompassing parties such as the Congress. Coalition politics in the central government has given state parties a toehold and a leverage point to defy these influences. In any case, the traditional structure of inter-governmental relations does not seem equipped to support the more subtle coordination that must happen in most areas where policy change is necessary.

Several essays in the book discuss options for formalizing a way for states' concerns to be represented and discussed in a productive way, rather than having centre–state disputes spill over into unproductive hold-ups in projects or policies.

By now the basic message of the book should be clear: India has some inherent advantages on the competitive playing field of the changing global economy, but we must build on these advantages with substantial reforms to succeed.

Some of the particular events or policies that the essays refer to may now seem slightly dated, but the underlying message—that much has changed, much more needs to change and that these changes are not easy in our institutional setting—is longer lasting. We must stay the course and allow 'the politics of change' to be a binding—not a divisive—influence in realizing our untapped growth potential.

I

GLOBALIZING INDIA

1

'Other' Superpowers Rising

Heraclitus once said that 'nothing endures but change' and this is especially true in the global economy. The centre of the world's economic gravity is moving east and south. The most recent *World Economic Outlook* (*WEO*) projects a world growth rate of about 4.1 per cent for 2004, while developing countries are expected to grow, on average, at 5.6 per cent. Developing and transitionary Asia is a particularly high-growth region, with conservative estimates of 5.9 per cent growth in India and 7.5 per cent in China next year.

Malaysia and Thailand are projected to grow at 5.3 per cent and 5.1 per cent respectively in 2004. Actual growth rates—both in India and China—have been way above the projections of the *WEO* with India in the current year poised to register 8 per cent growth and China growing at a somewhat faster rate. Vietnam is expected to grow by 7 per cent, while Bangladesh, another contributor to high Asia-region growth, is predicted to have a growth rate of 5.8 per cent.

The recent *Global Economic Prospects* (*GEP*) predicts mixed growth performance in Latin America next year but the longer-range expectations for large economies such as Brazil are more optimistic. Africa will also gain momentum. The *WEO* predicts an average growth rate of 5.6 per cent in 2004, though sub-Saharan Africa and Europe, in contrast, seem to be losing momentum, with adverse consequences for eastern and central European trading partners. A recent IMF report argues that United States' growing deficit is a potential threat to the world economy.

Overall, the predicted growth rate in the advanced economies, at 2.9 per cent, is substantially below the expected world average. And the future presents an even more marked shift: Brazil, Russia, India and China could have larger economies, in US dollar terms, than the G6 nations within forty years.

How will this new 'centre of gravity' affect the world economy? In simple terms, the dynamism of the Asian region cannot help but spill over to boost more general growth in the world economy. It seems clear that the trade transmission channel—in which fast-growing markets boost other nations' growth by acting as absorbers of exports—is only part of the way in which the new Asian economic powers will interact with the rest of the world. Growth in the developing Asian countries will also provide a source of high returns on investments, spilling over to increase incomes in slower-growing regions.

The new centre of gravity will perhaps introduce some stabilizing forces. One interesting possibility suggests that Asia's and other emerging markets' growth strategies will support wider growth in the world economy by continuing to finance the United States' deficit. It has been suggested that Asian countries' export-led growth strategies imply that exporting to the US is a key policy goal. The governments of these countries are thus willing to finance these exports by buying US securities if imports from the US fall short.

By their reasoning, this makes official creditors in Asia more willing to continue lending to the US even as the deficit grows and creditors who were solely interested in returns on their investments might demand a higher risk premium. While this might indeed be one aspect of the new international economy, I am somewhat sceptical of its sustainability. Recent analyses by Michael Dooley and others see no immediate end to this arrangement.

They anticipate (quite correctly) that Asia and other emerging economies have enough unrealized growth capacity to continue playing a large role in financing the US deficit. But they assume (possibly incorrectly) that these countries will continue to be single-mindedly interested in exporting to the US to the point that their governments will continue to be willing to hold US securities without demanding compensation for the additional risk due to growing deficits. The benefits of exporting to the US are decreasing while costs are increasing; at some point, the periphery will not finance the centre.

More importantly for our discussion, however, is the new gravitational force of large, underutilized labour pools in these new centres of gravity. Adjusting to the inevitable change in the location of economic activity and the transformation of industry within all globally integrated countries will be the biggest challenge we face. India and China's populations are the largest in the world, with Brazil, Indonesia, Pakistan and other developing countries not far behind. The US and Japan are the only two industrial countries among the top ten most populous nations.

Upcoming demographic changes reinforce this 'eastern centre of gravity'. The median age of the population in the Organization for Economic Cooperation and Development (OECD) countries is rising rapidly. The United States' labour force is expected to drop by seventeen million workers by 2020 and Japan's workforce by nine million over the same period. European demographics show a similar trend: France, Spain and Germany, for example, are each expected to have three million less workers in the labour force within the next two decades. India, in contrast, is expected to have forty-seven million more workers by 2020 and Pakistan, nineteen million more. Chinese and Russian demographics follow the OECD pattern of upcoming reductions in the labour force but most other developing and transition countries see labour force expansions.

The sheer number of workers alone already exerts a powerful attraction for the low-skill, manufacturing kinds of industries. As the skill base improves, however, more and more businesses are outsourcing call centres, back office operations as well as more sophisticated tasks like software creation and research and development. An accountant in the US costs $5,000 a month while one in India or Ireland costs $300. A chip designer in China, at a wage of $1000 a month, looks extremely appealing in comparison to her $7000-a-month counterpart in the US. Aerospace engineers in the Philippines cost little more than a tenth of the cost of aerospace engineers in the US. The relatively new phenomenon of clients going to where the service providers are is a second aspect of this shift in the location of economic activity.

The increasing number of patients from OECD countries seeking medical treatment and attention in India, Thailand and other Asian countries is a precursor of wider changes in other sectors. 'Nothing endures but change' in this kind of economy. The constant search for lower labour costs is already hollowing out manufacturing in many industrial countries. This phenomenon is not confined to the industrial countries.

In Mexico, for example, the maquiladora industry—essentially an outsourcing of US firms' lower-skilled manufacturing—was the top generator of hard currency in the late 1990s. More than a million workers were employed in foreign-owned plants in 2002 and 700 of the US *Fortune* 1000 companies had affiliates, component production, or some portion of their operations in Mexico during the same year. As workers' skills have improved, however, so has their productivity. With rising productivity come rising wages. Rising wages, in turn, prompted US firms to seek lower wage workers for the least skilled manufacturing jobs. Thus many maquiladora jobs moved to China and India.

Looking a decade or two forward, labour migrations will be an additional aspect of the reallocation of economic activity. The International Labour Organization (ILO) estimated that nearly fifty million foreign workers were already contributing to the European and US economies in 2002. While manufacturing and some services can be traded across countries, many other essential services cannot. There is growing recognition that ageing work forces in industrial countries will have to be supplemented, inevitably, by skilled and unskilled migrants from Asia and other emerging markets. There are several key factors in adjusting to this new global labour market.

The first is to increase funding for worker training to help them move higher up the manufacturing chain towards more skilled jobs. Sustainable expansion of jobs in the OECD depends on taking advantage of the education infrastructure to make sure that workers are ready for higher value added jobs as lower-skilled jobs continue to be pulled towards the new centres of gravity.

Second, financial markets must be ready to facilitate these labour-driven changes in the location of economic activities. Industrial countries should divert more funding into research and development to support the high-skilled industries that are these economies' comparative advantage. The priority for developing countries is flexibility, as these will be the nations climbing the skills ladder most quickly. Increasing financing for small and medium enterprises that can adjust to changing trends comparatively rapidly is one place to start.

Third, flexible immigration policies will be an important contributor to global growth. Migration has obvious benefits for sender countries—worker remittances have never been higher. The receiving countries benefit as well from lower labour costs, enhanced productivity and a fresh flow of ideas. These benefits will be all the more important as the dependency ratios of OECD countries increase and the costs of healthcare for ageing populations rise.

The United Nations recently launched the global commission on international migration which is one symbol of international commitment to developing a framework for migration; however, much of the impetus is on national policy-makers. The American response to increased outsourcing and rising migration (illegal and legal) is exactly the way not to adjust. Reduced visa quotas, particularly the H-1B visas reserved for highly-skilled workers are hurting many companies in the Silicon Valley. Various states' bills preventing the outsourcing of government practices are handicapping efforts to maintain the quality of social services while limiting growing budget deficits.

Finally, the markets emerging as the new centre of gravity also have their own set of adjustments to make. Weak protection for intellectual property rights still creates a deterrent to foreign investment and outsourcing, particularly in easy-to-replicate sectors such as pharmaceutical and technology components. However, the world would need to increasingly adjust to a new economic order with new centres of gravity. The preponderance of evidence and emerging trends inescapably point in this direction. This will only be reinforced by the negative ways in which the emerging trends are being handled by the present centres of economic power. Whether it is the negatives or the positives, the centre of economic gravity is certainly shifting and must adjust to the new realities.

Postscript

Global growth has continued unabated. The figures for 2006 suggest a growth rate of 3.6 per cent, somewhat lower than in 2004 but nonetheless a period of continued global buoyancy. The growth rate in Asia continues to be high. Notwithstanding fears of a global slowdown, the medium-term outlook continues to be reasonably optimistic.

Alan Greenspan's comment that it was possible but improbable for the US to go into a recession has once again raised issues connected with global structural imbalances. While the US has improved its fiscal deficit, its current account deficit continues to be large and the probability of how long Asia will continue to finance consumption in the US remains debatable. There is even more evidence of a shift in the centre of economic gravity towards Asia. However, the impact of rising wage rates and inadequate investment in human resource development may limit the pace of outsourcing.

The debate on international migration lacks coherent focus. The report of the United Nations' global commission on international migration led to a high-level dialogue but follow-up on several controversial issues remains weak. The key issues on migration remain grounded in politics.

20 February 2004

2

Get Fleet-footed at Davos

Davos 2007 is behind us. Over the years this annual meeting of the World Economic Forum has continued to generate debates on contemporary issues ranging from global growth, poverty, development in Africa, terrorism, Iraq, and now, climate change.

Heads of state and government, policy makers, academics and, of course, the corporate world have been more than generous in successively participating in these events. The Indian contingent to Davos has many faithfuls—veterans like Rahul Bajaj, Dhruv Sahini and Tarun Das have been going there for twenty-five years. I began going to Davos only in the late nineties and even over this period, the forum has changed significantly.

One, responding to persistent criticism that it was being increasingly perceived as an elitist club, it broadened participation by including people from civil society, art and culture, physical and spiritual well-being. This has both enlarged and altered the profile of the participants. One unhappy outcome of this is that it has lost its earlier character and has become too big for intimate networking. On the other hand, one has more to choose.

Two, it realized that economic pursuit is pointless without political engagement. Issues of security are part of societal well-being. The enhanced presence of important political leaders across continents and ideologies has now made the interactions between politics and economics more meaningful.

Three, it has strengthened its regional footprints. The Annual Asia

Summit (the next one is in Singapore), the China Meet and the India Summit along with a robust programme for young global leaders have closely focused on country-specific questions and lent synergy to the annual Davos meet.

So, to the somewhat rhetorical question of whether Davos has lost its relevance in a more integrated world, one can respond that Davos has instead readapted and constantly seeks to rediscover its relevance both by changing issues, the format and the profile of its participants.

Is Davos still meaningful from India's point of view? I remember that in the mid-nineties, when our reforms were still tentative, passionate pleas, the irreversibility of the changes needed constant reiteration. While it made some dent on investors, there were nagging doubts on the sustainability of our initiatives.

All this has changed dramatically. Not only has our recent economic performance silenced many critics, it has ensured that India is not an unknown entity any more. Investors we meet in Davos are more frequently to be found in India. Apart from complimenting us on our progress they actively seek new opportunities, are broadening their earlier engagement and are more concerned about the sequencing and pace of our changes. Doubts do persist on whether coalition politics will permit the many reforms waiting to happen, but given the track record of successive governments no one fears any reversal or serious setbacks.

The tardy liberalization of our financial and banking sectors continues to be a matter of concern. While everyone recognizes that infrastructure is improving in civil aviation as well as the telecom sector, the same cannot be said about the power sector.

The many clearances required to set up new businesses and the time it took to get approval at each step were still irritants and the concept of single-window clearance continues to be elusive. Also bothersome to many are tardy changes in many state governments, as well as issues of centre–state relations. On the whole, while the marketing of India may be substantially over, the challenge of enticing investments is still a long haul.

From India's point of view, Davos may have changed from a marketing venue to an investment venue. Globally speaking, there is still no other meet that attracts so many investors and therefore sector-specific investment proposals and fixing meetings well in advance will give us multiple benefits. We need to leverage Davos more strategically in seeking such investments and bring in state governments in a bigger way.

At the recent Davos meeting, the panels and workshops, numbering over 200, covered many facets of our society. Of course, the focus was on bridging the divides, with considerable attention paid to climate change.

Let me comment on the special session, 'Asian Brainstorming', to consider issues of relevance to this rapidly growing part of the world. Interestingly, based on surveys and discussions, the priority concerns centred on the absence of regional institutions to discuss energy, security and the environment.

There were worries on the impact of Indian and Chinese growth on the future competitiveness of some countries in the region. Among the risk management factors, the big worry, even more than oil price shock and fears of the avian flu, was of corruption at local levels.

Many of these themes also mirror India's concerns. The prime minister has repeatedly commented on the need to strengthen the Asian economic community and seek a cooperative framework beyond preferential trade agreements. The development of an Asian currency unit may be a far cry, but managing the economic consequences of an ageing population in Japan, Korea and China is something that needs attending to at once.

The Asia focus is now a common global theme. Davos continues to reinvent its agenda to reflect contemporary challenges.

4 February 2007

3

Tuning in to Global Risks

Given the prevalent economic euphoria, any suggestion about risks, much less global risks, can be viewed as undue pessimism. Everyone now regards inflation as an immediate problem and improving infrastructure as well as the regulatory environment as ongoing concerns.

No doubt, continued global prosperity over the last five years and a buoyant outlook in the near term have contributed to our competitiveness and enhanced financial flows. The increasing integration of our economy makes us both a beneficiary and a victim of exogenous events.

Global risks have received fragmented attention. A report titled 'Global Risks 2007', prepared by the World Economic Forum in collaboration with the Wharton School Risk Centre, Swiss Re, Marsh & McLennan Companies and CitiGroup, advocates the active engagement of all sections of the international community in dealing with these risks because no one group has the ability to effectively mitigate them.

The core global risks have been divided into five broad categories. The economic risks include oil price shocks, energy supply interruptions, a fiscal crisis caused by demographic shifts, Chinese economic hard landing and disorderly adjustment to present structural imbalances.

The environmental risks reflect the current concerns about climate change, loss of freshwater services and heightened natural catastrophes, particularly tropical storms and inland flooding.

The societal risks include pandemics, infectious diseases in the developing world and chronic diseases in the developed world along with associated technological concerns, particularly the breakdown of critical information infrastructure and risks associated with nanotechnology.

There are serious geo-political concerns about international terrorism, Mid-East instability, proliferation of weapons of mass destruction, mass retrenchment from globalization and the problems of failed and failing states.

Second, issues concerning global warming and climate change have been described in a scenario called 'Out of the Global Warming Frying Pan (and into the Fiscal Fire).'

Third, 'Oil Shock and its Consequences' focuses on the disorderly changes and economic activities in the search for alternative energy forms and the serious transition costs.

Fourth, the financial and human consequences relating to heightened security concerns, some of which we are now familiar with.

It is interesting that while greater awareness can mitigate risks, the existence of heuristics biases distort our ability to assess risks effectively. Our decisions 'frequently depend on approximations of the world around us—short cuts that allow quick decisions while resorting to learned behaviours.' Policy errors in risk management can arise in multiple ways including heuristics, which can both mitigate and exacerbate them.

The report suggests that research, enhancing information inflows, refocusing incentives to mitigate risk and improving investment in such areas are important and the creation of an institutional framework will greatly improve the coherence of our response.

It also suggests two 'institutional innovations' to manage global risks. The first is to designate a single country risk officer who can prioritize risk on a cross-sectoral basis, explore private-sector techniques assessment, management and transference.

The second is to facilitate the setting up of a 'coalition of the willing', which will regard 'individual global risks involving different groups of countries in a system of flexible geometry'.

A global risk management institute will help in networking and facilitate meaningful dialogue among experts in varied sectors cutting across specialized boundaries. The institute could also create a close network of experts pursuing an interdisciplinary approach in forecasting, evaluating and mitigating risk.

I venture to suggest that India could be a preferred location for such an institute given its demography, high vulnerability to multiple global risks and a talent pool in the many disciplines which may be involved.

No doubt such an institute could become a robust example of successful private–public partnership.

18 February 2007

4

Investors: The 'Take off' and 'Landing' Mode

The prime minister's first visit to the UK and the US after he assumed office was preceded by a flurry of activity. The cabinet approved the promulgation of three ordinances pertaining to banking regulation (amendment and miscellaneous provisions), Securities Contract (Regulations) Act, 1956, as well as the Depositories Act, 1996, apart from deciding to set up a competitiveness commission. Officials habitually use prime ministerial visits to push through pending decisions believing that this will improve investor perceptions. All prime ministers are susceptible to this. When their aircraft are in the 'take-off mode', the investor constituency becomes more compelling, just as on return, when the aircraft is in the 'landing mode', domestic concerns and political compulsions once again dominate their thought processes.

Given the present prime minister's professional integrity and high international credibility, it is not surprising that he was a big hit with CEOs both in London and New York. Shortly after the prime minister's return to India, the finance minister would also be interacting with merchant bankers and the investing community both in New York and London, after participating in the annual meeting of the IMF and World Bank in Washington. The 'India Roadshow' has got off to a mega start; in quick succession, the international business community would have interfaced with the prime minister and the finance minister of the new government.

So what are the prospects?

Firstly, we must recognize that even after more than a decade of significant market liberalization, FDI annual flows hover around $4-5 billion depending on the methodology we use to compute these figures. This is quite abysmal. This is even more so because on the whole, India has a credible record in terms of the GDP growth it has achieved during the 1990s. There has been significant infrastructure deregulation, particularly in the telecom and roads sectors, coupled with a modest degree of banking and financial sector reforms. The present economic environment is stable and attractive. The macro-fundamentals look reasonably healthy with the assurance that the fiscal deficit target is likely to be achieved, tax revenues are buoyant, market borrowings are lower than anticipated, inflation may have peaked and the external sector looking up. Along with these is the prime minister's repeated assurance that 'reforms with a human face' (whatever that means—different prime ministers use different phrases at different points of time depending on the constituency they want to address) are firmly on track. So what are the persisting concerns of investors?

a) Coalition politics will hurt economic reforms. Every day we hear discordant voices both from coalition partners in the government and outside. While the prime minister reassures us that the government is committed to decisions that have been taken, the proof of the pudding lies in the eating.
b) Budget proposals relating to sector caps on telecom and civil aviation have yet to be notified. Nor has the cabinet approved the proposal on raising the FDI cap on insurance from 26 to 49 per cent, much less introduce a bill in parliament. We hear there will be more discussions on these. Is there much left to be discussed since arguments and concerns, the pros and cons have been thoroughly discussed and are in the public domain? Chidambaram is not naive enough to believe that the removal of these caps will lead to a burst of foreign investment from the very next day, but these are symbolic of the credibility of the government in implementing its own decisions, taken consciously. Fullest consultations/consensus should precede announcement; but policies once announced must be implemented. Beyond sector cap, the issue of policies, procedures

and promotion of foreign investment needs to be holistically addressed. The same is true of airport privatization and power sector reforms. Actually there has been a slide back. Foreign equity in airports was brought down from 74 to 49 per cent, and there is yet no final clarity on whether we are going ahead even with the newly visualized joint venture agreement, though ten parties have been shortlisted and the date extended by another few months. On power sector reforms, the classic issue of application of user charges, moderating the cross-subsidy to tolerable levels which do not render manufacturing activity uncompetitive along with finality about the Electricity Act and its follow-up in terms of the national electricity policy and tariff policy will keep the investing community confused.

c) Other issues continue to haunt investors. The unresolved Enron problem; the issue of resiling on banking liberalization; on removing the 10 per cent cap on voting rights decided by the earlier government and raising the foreign equity cap to 74 per cent. Further, how are we to improve the cost and quality of infrastructure? Excepting the telecom sector, the cost of most infrastructures is 50–100 per cent higher than in China. The Chinese highway network is seven times larger than India with China spending 2.5 per cent of its GDP in improving highways. The total freight payment in Indian ports is 11 per cent of import value, compared to a global average of just 5 per cent.
A clearer enunciation of our disinvestment policy—perhaps a roadmap or a timeframe—will lend comfort to the hapless lot of merchant bankers attempting to second guess the next move by the government. Issues pertaining to inculcation of labour skills and improving labour productivity also figure high on investor concerns.

d) The government was perhaps left with no option but to promulgate some ordinances since the parliament has hardly enacted any legislation during the last budget session. These ordinances would need to be converted into bills. But will the bills be passed? And what will be the fate of several other important legislations in the offing? Investors would like to believe that the breakfast meeting on Pakistan between the prime minister and his predecessor is the

> beginning of wider cooperation between the two mainstream parties on crucial economic issues. Unless this is achieved, important legislation will remain in limbo as the government's flexibility is greatly circumscribed. Besides, there are limits beyond which the ordinance route cannot be pursued. How does one achieve this? This is an important question with no clear answers.

Hopefully, after the elections in Maharashtra, there may be 'a window of opportunity' to secure greater understanding between the government and the opposition. But alas, this window would be short-lived because then we will have the Bihar elections and so on! We have elections almost round the year and, clearly, bipartisan cooperation must look beyond the arithmetic of constant elections in one form or the other.

The prime minister is right in reminding the foreign investor community of what Keynes has said describing 'investment as an act of faith'. While this is true, Keynes had also said that 'the social object of skilled investment should be to defeat the dark forces of time and ignorance which envelop our future'. No 'act of faith' can be sustained without trust and credibility. Can we be 'faithful' enough in keeping promises made and implementing decisions announced? Actions always speak louder than words and this must not be forgotten in the 'landing mode'.

26 September 2004

5

Consolidating the Gains

Jaipur, one of India's prime tourist destinations, recently played host to a high-profile investors' conference. The tenth India Investors' Conference, organized by Merrill Lynch, witnessed the presence of global institutional investors in what was described as 'sixty-two presentations over five days at Jaipur'. Two years ago, while addressing a similar conference in Udaipur, I interacted with a modest number of fifty participants. This year, the number exceeded 150 and as chairman, DSP Merrill Lynch, Hemendra Kothari explained, a large number of participants had to be turned away due to paucity of rooms. Against a minimum requirement of 250 rooms they could cobble together just 180 rooms. The paucity of hotel rooms in India is a serious constraint in attracting worthwhile international events but that subject deserves separate treatment. The timing of the conference, just after the Sensex had breached the psychological barrier of 10,000, and the recently released upbeat GDP figures suggesting 8 per cent growth had already buoyed investor sentiments. The participants at the conference were resource rich, enthusiastic about India and not the complaining lot which all of us have encountered many a time. The one-to-one investor meet which is customary and also one of the more productive aspects of such a conference saw the presence of most Indian majors like ONGC, Reliance, Infosys, Bharti, TISCO, Ranbaxy, Jet Airways and L&T to name a few. So what has changed in the last two or three years?

Firstly, expectations. There is renewed confidence that the India success story is a sustainable one and the perceived risks rather low. Earlier, such meetings invariably had a daunting wishlist on unfinished reforms, policy infirmities, regulatory opaqueness and the familiar bureaucratic and procedural irritants. This time around the wishlist was not of constraints but of opportunities. Investors were busy with potential India partners in delineating emerging opportunities. There was seriousness in their intent and an anxiety to not miss the present Indian boom cycle.

Secondly, the continuity of the reform momentum in multiple directions is now generally accepted. Roads are getting better, civil aviation is quickly opening up with airport modernization in sight, telecom is a runaway success even though the power sector remains worrisome. Visible progress and the government saying all the right things (not all of which they have translated into practice) coupled with significant success in forging strategic alliances with the USA along with improved relations with China and the ASEAN countries have made a decisive psychological difference.

Third, institutional investors are by temperament somewhat wary of green-fields or long-gestation-period projects. They prefer listed companies and a diversification strategy where risks are better hedged. That is why the one-to-one with leading Indian corporate houses was a productive exercise. In the medium term, there was strong interest in urban townships, the transport and construction sector, the special economic zones and participation in special purpose vehicles with possible access to the recently created viability gap funding mechanism. The research team of Merrill Lynch outlined its '10 Thoughts for India 2006' on market and economy. These included the following: To view 2006 as a year of consolidation which will see some volatility in markets after a one-way bullish trend with their movement being closely correlated to all emerging global markets. The economic momentum would be sustained by a continuation of the consumption cycle and notwithstanding rising interest rates, higher infrastructure spending will be the big driver of economic growth. Upward movement in interest rates to mitigate inflationary expectations with rising current account deficit and slowing down of reserve accretion will be part of the scenario. In the pleasant surprises there is expectation that post-Assembly elections in West Bengal, Kerala, Assam, Tamil Nadu and Pondicherry, there will be greater willingness on the part of the allies to support reform initiatives. A possible fall in oil prices would help lower interest rates and ease fears of inflation. The enactment of the pension fund reforms could trigger large-scale investment in equities. Of course, there are worries that because India has been a major beneficiary of FII flows over the past three years, a significant change in the global liquidity environment could see the reversal of these flows.

No doubt, all this optimism assumes purposeful action. A budget without excessive populism, return to fiscal rectitude, sharp reduction in tariffs to align with ASEAN rates, continuation of a regime of moderate tax rates with administrative and procedural simplification (abstaining from clever but unfriendly irritants), introduction of the promised legislation on raising the insurance cap, early passage of the Pension Bill, tangible action (not promises) on banking reforms and flexibility in labour policies are necessary preconditions for a continuation of the current bullish sentiment. Policy makers need not be wary of shifting goalposts. After all we have now reached a new threshold. However, we need not lament either if 2006 turns out to be a year of consolidation.

12 February 2006

6

Preferential Trade Agreements: Stumbling Blocks or Building Blocks

India seems to have fully embraced the new paradigm of Preferential Trade Agreements (PTAs). The report of the India–China joint study group presented to the two prime ministers embarks us on the complex endeavour of a India–China PTA or preferably a comprehensive economic cooperation agreement (CECA). The CECA with Singapore is round the corner. We have also commenced negotiations with the Mercosur group comprising Brazil, Argentina, Uruguay and Paraguay.

Negotiations with Thailand are underway as also with the ASEAN countries based on the framework agreement. The share of international trade under preferential access conditions now exceeds 55 per cent. The European Union and the NAFTA having led the way in creating large trading blocks have spurred others along the same path. India's effort to enhance its trade profile deserves encouragement. While India's trade to GDP ratio following policy changes since 1991 might have increased significantly, yet, according to the world development indicators, it was still around 32 per cent (31.76 per cent to be exact) of the GDP in 2003. This is less than the figure of 25 per cent contained in the RBI report. However, adhering to the World Development Index (WDI) data, there are only three countries that had a lower trade–GDP ratio in 2003, namely Syria, Burundi and Sudan. India was narrowly beaten by Burkina Faso in terms of trade–GDP ratio and even by Bangladesh which has a trade–GDP ratio of 34.02 per cent. These figures are surprising in the context of the popular applause on our trade performance. Of course, our export–import volume is much larger but when expressed as a percentage of the GDP, our achievement appears modest.

As India hurtles towards more preferential arrangements, some basic issues remain unresolved. Why are we finding PTAs more attractive than non-discriminatory multilateral arrangements? Is this because PTAs are smaller, any opening is partial and thus seemingly less threatening to domestic interests? Or that they do not create 'transitional shocks' to domestic interest groups even though productivity and efficiency enhancement would remain more limited. Are we entering into these PTAs believing that some liberalization is better than no liberalization? And partial opening is superior to protectionism.

Any evaluation would suggest that PTAs have the following advantages:

- PTAs are one form of trade agreements and beneficial in optimizing comparative advantages.
- PTAs are politically more feasible and can be implemented without excessive opposition from domestic manufacturers.
- They enhance the size of the market, improve externalities with consequent improvement in efficiency and productivity which are irreversible.
- They result in greater flow of direct foreign investment among the member states. They improve the level of confidence between contracting authorities allaying in some cases subsisting security concerns. Enhanced trade and economic interdependence are important ingredients of confidence-building measures.
- Finally, they create a framework for expanding the size of the preferential trade and eventual merger within a multilateral framework.

In contrast the negatives are equally compelling:

- Empirical evidence suggests that the PTAs have not created the same kind of productivity increases as multilateral arrangements; they distort trade patterns between members and non-members building on incentives for inefficient specialization.

- The additional production encouraged by PTAs may not be internationally competitive at current prices; the arrangement might result in existing industry becoming less competitive—national welfare gains from even country-driven reforms may be greater than improved market access and thus become an inefficient way to transfer income to the poor.
- Investments which become irreversible commit countries to trading with each other and create inefficient structures which may not subsequently withstand global competition.
- The alliance between PTA countries could create stronger protectionist lobbies which may be more difficult to dismantle; these protectionist groups may also become politically more formidable. By locking a country into an inefficient production pattern, they handicap its ability to adjust to a structure that would be more competitive under global free trade. A country is better off joining a PTA where its position relative to other members is similar to its comparative advantage to the rest of the world and so specialization is similar to what would occur in general trade.

So what does this mean from India's point of view? Given our tariff structure, which is relatively higher than all other countries in the region, trade advantages for us, per se, are not particularly attractive. However, if such preferential arrangements become part of a larger economic package which covers investment, services, freer movement of skilled manpower, it would make an assessment more complex.

These agreements should then be considered not so much in terms of how much trade liberalization they bring or how to value this liberalization relative to multilateral trade liberalization but rather in terms of the benefits of larger investments, technical cooperation, immigration agreements and their multiplier effect. Our high GDP growth and a rapidly growing middle class with rising incomes, both in the urban and rural sector for white and brown goods, are strong incentives to other countries seeking a slice from this expanding market.

Nonetheless, from India's point of view, preferential trade arrangements cannot be a substitute for multilateral trade liberalization. We cannot promote arrangements for nations to get embedded in what Anne Kruger describes as the 'spaghetti bowl of mutually inconsistent trade restrictions'. These agreements will hopefully induce faster alignment with average peak and applied ASEAN tariff rates.

Such arrangements must be evaluated in terms of encouraging much greater investment flows, improving labour productivity and skills in sectors where our comparative factor advantage remains unrealized. Their long-term value lie in spurring faster overall policy changes and adopting the best international practices on fiscal policy, tax regimes, labour laws, treatment of foreign investment and environmental regulations to name a few. Only then can PTAs become a 'building block' and not a 'stumbling block' for faster development processes.

Postscript

The comprehensive economic cooperation agreement with Singapore was finalized in June 2005. However, its implementation has raised some issues which are yet to be fully resolved.

The larger debate on the value of a preferential trade agreement versus a multilateral arrangement remains wide open. The Doha Round on a new multilateral trade agreement (the so-called development round) remains stalled even though there are optimistic noises. There is also uncertainty on whether the fast track authority by the US Congress which expires in July this year will be renewed.

In the meantime India continues to pursue PTAs with several Asian countries and its efforts to align its tariff structure with the ASEAN region will facilitate this process. Nonetheless, creating sub-optimal economic activity could mitigate in future against alignments with multilateral arrangements. The slogan that 'some progress is better than no progress' continues to resonate in the writings of economists and journalists.

24 April 2005

7

Tenets of Economic Diplomacy

As India's economy gathers strength and the world becomes increasingly integrated, economic diplomacy assumes importance. This was recognized by the prime minister in his early days in office and the constitution of a high-level committee on international economic relations was one positive outcome. In the first four decades of independence, we were preoccupied with seeking food security and with managing our vulnerable balance of payments. This needed successful bilateral diplomacy and bolstering support for the Aid India consortium under the leadership of the World Bank. Having successfully achieved these ends, it is only from the mid-1990s that high growth rates, rising foreign exchange reserves, continued economic liberalization and a quest for foreign investment altered our strategy.

So what should be the tenets of economic diplomacy?

- First and foremost, as part of the broader foreign policy strategy, it must serve overall strategic interest; managing the neighbours, meeting defence requirements, securing energy security or promoting India's legitimate claim to a place on the UN Security Council.
- Second, it must meet the needs of a growing exporting community and in a broader sense strengthen our position in multilateral fora even while seeking the best terms for preferential trade agreements.

- Third, actively promote India as a profitable destination for foreign investment even as liberalization enlarges opportunity and we seek resources and high quality knowledge capital to enhance competitive efficiency.
- Fourth, promote the unique brand India in seeking investment, attracting tourism, encouraging business outsourcing and a multitude of connected economic activities.
- Fifth, as Indian corporates have become globally competitive and seek avenues for overseas investments to service their complex needs, build a credible database, secure its dissemination, make effective interlocution with foreign governments, assist in overcoming legal obstacles and in resolution of disputes which may arise.
- Finally, make strategic investments beyond neighbouring countries in other emerging markets to enhance prestige and fortify leadership in the developing world. This goes beyond aid and includes investment in infrastructure, enhanced technical cooperation and human resource development to name a few.

Do we have the institutional mechanism for these objectives? Perhaps not. Indian diplomats are second to none and barring exceptions, have effectively used their meagre resources to meet multifarious demands. No doubt, for decades, economic work had low priority. This has changed. However, missions abroad are generally overstretched both for manpower and resources. Barring some cases, representational grants are grossly inadequate to meet these new demands; a significant proportion is spent in servicing visiting delegations.

A tangible plan of action would need to include:

- The budget of the ministry of external affairs (MEA) needs a second look. The MEA's expenditure as a percentage of the national budget is around 0.75 per cent compared to 2.15 per cent in Canada, 1.3 per cent in New Zealand, over 1 per cent in Singapore and is significantly lower than many other countries. What is worse is the ratio of staffing of Indian missions compared to the strength of the ministry itself; a poor 1:4 compared to the international average of 1:1.5. So first and foremost, the budget as a whole and the proportion between missions abroad and the ministry need correction.

- The centrality or the goalkeeper role of the foreign office has been greatly eroded. Initiatives have been taken by various ministries. However, the coordinative role of the MEA which can synergize the efforts of the ministries of economic affairs, commerce, petroleum needs to be re-established. This can be achieved without transferring functions but through vastly improved interdepartmental coordinative mechanisms. The reorganization of the foreign office involves reorganization of the commerce and economic affairs departments as well. In the case of the commerce ministry, while we need not replicate the United States Trade Representatives (USTR), which has a distinguished array of legal experts; the meagre resources of the trade policy division is pathetic. Similarly, if the department of economic affairs is to be nodal in catalysing both domestic economic reforms and attracting foreign investment, it needs reorganization and strengthening in critical areas.
- Reorganizing the work of the Indian missions themselves entails developing high-quality database as well as improving the quality of personnel by their secondment from specialized organizations like the CII or other trade bodies. The foreign office, both at headquarters and in critical missions abroad, can scarcely ignore the need to induct talent and expertise and invest in human resource development. We need to learn best practices from countries which have made a successful transaction.

The distractions of coalition politics have left the prime minister little time for improving governance. Any credible exercise must include reorganization of ministries and departments themselves. The foreign office in tandem with some other economic ministries whose activities have an international dimension need refocus and reorganization. The prime minister is currently the foreign minister as well. This is a time when directions can be given and action initiated to make economic diplomacy symmetrical with the emerging perception of India as the new upcoming economic powerhouse.

20 November 2005

8

Taking the French Connection beyond Wine and Cheese

I am in Paris to speak at the second conference on India organized by the Indo-French Association (AFUI), being held at the French senate under the patronage of its president, Christian Poncelet. This is the second time that I would be speaking to a distinguished audience of senators, business representatives and a diverse segment of French society. The conference is designed to look at India in a composite way from the viewpoint of economic progress, technological changes, cultural roots, legal framework and even Bollywood. So what, broadly, are the opportunities and constraints in furthering Indo–French relations, particularly those arising from new economic opportunities? Relations in the recent past have not suffered any serious political irritants. The impression that we have not adequately reciprocated their support on a wide range of issues like membership of the Security Council or for not ostracizing us following the nuclear tests needs correction.

Mechanisms like round table conferences, strategic dialogues and visits of political dignitaries from both sides have helped mutual understanding. Nonetheless, economic engagement remains tentative. French businessmen are influenced by a positive coverage of India in financial and economic spheres and want an Indian presence or upgraded exposure, but cannot fully get over their initial hesitation.

The hangover of past anecdotal irritants must be put to rest. The investment community, banks and financial institutions need aggressive engagement. Consider the following:

On bilateral trade, while France is our fifth trading partner among the EU countries; our total trade is just over US $2.3 billion with exports from India worth US $1.2 billion while imports are just over $1 billion. Only 2.3 per cent of our global exports (which itself is rather small) go to France and only 1.3 per cent of our total imports are sourced from them. India's share in France's global imports is 0.45 per cent lower than even our low share of global trade. On investment, the numbers are equally small. The total approved foreign direct investment (FDI) from France is US $1.72 billion, which is just 3 per cent of the FDI approved from all countries.

Actual flows are also at just 3 per cent.

The initiation of a strategic dialogue with France was a qualitative gain. While the outcome in economic spheres remains opaque, one must not unmask the mystique of strategic dialogues. Shorn of mystique they would be so mundane!

Here are some suggestions:

The total number of Indian students who annually secure admission in France is just 500. Compare this to 15,000 for the UK and 70,000 for the USA! An important barrier is language. The French government has extended the reach and penetration of the Alliance Francaise in India. This may not be enough. Universities need to undertake special programmes for imparting language skills and the corporate sector and bodies like the CII need to support through scholarship programmes. We have resumed the acceptance of French assistance after a short, ill-thought-out interruption. These resources can partly fund language progammes. An increase in the number of Indian students in French universities has multiplier benefits. On investment opportunities in India, clearly, there is scope for much greater expansion. Interminable delays like aircraft acquisition, submarine or Mirage purchases add to the discomfort.

While inter-firm and inter-company awareness in France continues to be weak, there is expanding scope in sectors like energy, particularly power and nuclear energy and water management to name a few. With depleting fossil fuel-based energy and given India's demographic and development compulsion for high energy needs, dependence on nuclear energy has considerable advantages. In the short run, seeking enhanced French cooperation for increasing nuclear energy availability is high priority. In the medium term, no doubt, we need to harness thermo-nuclear energy as discussed at the recent EU Summit. 1,00,000 MW of power from nuclear (later thermo-nuclear sources) may sound ambitious but would make a qualitative difference to our development process. The joint working groups must finalize some tangible projects, preferably with French equity or as joint ventures, since in several areas, particularly power and atomic energy, public sectors are either nodal or dominant.

In agriculture, the moderation of high subsidies would make France an attractive market for Indian farm products. There are converse opportunities as well. The French, notwithstanding competition, have retained their reputation in wine cultivation. However, duty on wine continues to be a punitive 180 per cent, adding both central and state levies. Moderate wine drinking, particularly of red wine, is receiving favourable health reviews. Duty moderation, apart from benefiting Indian consumers, would create a climate for joint ventures in wine cultivation in areas where soil conditions are favourable.

On agro-processing, the multiplicity of our food laws will inhibit any investor. It does not help if Perrier water, consumed in over 130 countries, is declared as being contaminated in India! A group of ministers constituted two years ago to draft a food legislation is still deliberating. More than the laws themselves the debate is about who should enforce the laws—food inspectors are not reconciled to losing this high-rent territory.

If India needs to wake up, so do the French. French banks like BNP Paribas or Société Générale are nowhere near matching the aggressiveness of their American counterparts in grasping opportunities in private banking including retail banking.

Similarly, in areas like automobile or auto ancillary, consumer durables, mining and metallurgy, the scope available to the French industry remains grossly underutilized. Indian corporates are aggressively seeking acquisitions abroad to synergize their existing operations or diversify product and process activities. France offers interesting possibilities for Indian corporate investment.

Raymond Barre, the former French prime minister, at a meeting of ASPEN France enquired from me as to when the rush of Indian students to the trans-Atlantic shores would help Europe secure a fair share of professionals. Security concerns might limit access to the US and a saturation point with the UK may soon be reached. We must diversify our linkages and seek new opportunities.

The French can help us, and in the process help themselves, by making it less difficult for Indian professionals to secure work permits. Fortunately, positive developments in India have not gone unnoticed and a number of joint projects in the pipeline could reach a critical mass in the near future. Indo-French relations must look beyond culinary delights—wine and cheese or curry and biryani. Just like 'nouveau cuisine' is a fusion cuisine where we readapt our food habits, the dimensions of our relations must readapt to the new economic realities.

28 November 2004

II

INDIA AND CHINA

9

The Battle for Knowledge Economy

The new aggressiveness of India and China in capitalizing on their demographic advantages, particularly in high-quality knowledge-intensive and innovative enterprises has caused concerns elsewhere. The worry is highest in the United States. The report of a high-level committee titled 'Rising Above the Gathering Storm—Energizing and Employing America for a Brighter Economic Future' has made far-reaching recommendations on reversing a trend where the dilution of comparative advantages in knowledge-intensive and innovative enterprises will hurt economic leadership.

The report must be seen in the backdrop of what is described as 'worrisome indicators'. These include facts like fewer than one-third of US fourth- and eighth-grade students performing at a level called 'proficient' in mathematics and twelfth graders performing below the international average for twenty-one countries in mathematics and science. While America produced 70,000 engineers in 2004, China graduated over 6,00,000 with India producing 3,50,000. A slackening of money spent on research and development (R & D) with US industry spending more on litigation than on R&D is also worrisome.

In the light of the aforesaid, the committee has made four basic recommendations to focus on human, financial and knowledge capital for US prosperity which cover action on education (10,000 teachers, ten million minds), research sowing the seeds, higher education (best and brightest) and sustaining innovation. The action plan includes significantly increased recruitment of teachers in science and mathematics, crash courses in sciences, attractive financial incentives for faculty, researchers and students, and generous student scholarships which can prevent further haemorrhaging.

Additional action has also been proposed for incentives for innovation and improved investment environment which enhances intellectual property(IP) protection and reforms in the working of the patents and trademark office.

How should India respond to these new initiatives? A 'Knowledge Commission' was launched in early August to advise the prime minister on 'matters relating to institutions of knowledge production, knowledge housing to be removed and knowledge dissemination and ideas designed to sharpen India's knowledge edge'. Speaking on the occasion, the prime minister emphasized that harnessing our brain power was crucial for sustaining the country's economic competitiveness.

There are really two issues with the knowledge economy: education and human resources development to produce good researchers on the one hand and IP protection and R&D funding to encourage these good researchers to produce useful knowledge on the other.

On human resource development, basically, any strategy to develop a broader base of researchers has to address both the demand and the supply side of education.

Students must want to learn and to make the sacrifices required. They need to want to study the subjects that will propel the national knowledge economy forward, because they see personal returns. Parents need to see the value of being supportive.

The demand side has been eroded in the US as well and to some extent in India by low-quality schooling. Citizens in both countries have limited access to the best education at all levels. While the demand for quality education is clearly present (the number of students competing for entrance to IITs and IIMs, or the US Ivy Leagues is one indicator), demand for the average education available is not as strong.

Most policy prescriptions (the 'Gathering Storm' and Knowledge Commission) focus on the supply side.

This is appropriate—it is needed, especially in India where teacher absenteeism is a problem and the student–teacher ratio is increasing. But simply expanding the supply—more buildings, more teachers—however, is not going to improve educational outcomes in the long run. Perhaps this is easier, but what would make students take advantage of these expanded facilities?

Improving supply will entail:

- Paying teachers and academics more so that the profession becomes more attractive and not just a last resort for those who cannot find other jobs or have an unusual altruism;
- Taking advantage of IT to share knowledge, and for distance learning; and
- Incorporating internships and other real-world experience into the classroom and education sequence.

With regard to intellectual protection, there are two basic ways to reward research: ex-ante funding and ex-post rewards. The American report addresses both, while the Indian report focuses more on the latter.

Both are complicated by the same basic question: how do you observe and reward the process of research? Ex-ante rewards will only produce good outcomes if they reward 'good' researchers, but who are 'good' researchers? Ex-post rewards have a different issue: the 'good' researchers have already identified themselves by producing something, but then the question is how much to reward them.

Balancing these two demands is also complicated by the fact that research effort cannot be rewarded directly, because it is not observable. How to get around this, or at least to find the most socially and economically efficient trade-off, remains, however, the unresolved priority question.

13 November 2005

10

Watch Out, India Is Only Revving Up (Part 1 of Two Part Series)

A horse never runs so fast as when he has other horses to catch up with and outpace — Ovid

Would it be reasonable to suggest that given China's spectacular growth achievements, India has been spurred to policy changes necessary for accelerating its own growth momentum? The India–China comparison has been made many times and almost ad nauseum. Nonetheless, it needs to be recognized that while India hesitatingly undertook tentative reforms in 1980, serious reforms only began in 1991. This process, however, has gathered momentum over the past five years.

On the other hand, China's serious reforms started at least a decade earlier, around 1977–78. Consequentially, with the acceleration of its growth rate, rural poverty fell from 30.7 per cent in 1979 to 4.6 per cent in 1998. World Bank estimates of rural poverty changes from 40.8 per cent in 1990 to 24.2 per cent in 1997 show a similar trend (though at very different levels).

The gap between India and China widened significantly over the 1970s and the early 1980s. While the Indian growth rate over 1950–80 was around 3.5 per cent per year, China's economy is estimated to have grown at 4.5 per cent per year.

India has not yet caught up with China's 'headstart'. Nonetheless, India's reforms in the 1980s and 1990s did bring about significant improvement on social indicators: the incidence of poverty fell from 44.5 per cent in the 1980s to 26.1 per cent in 2000 while the literacy rate increased from 44 per cent to 65 per cent and life expectancy rose from fifty-six to sixty-one years over the same time period.

Policy changes also led to an increased growth rate, from the 3 per cent 'Hindu rate of growth' to 5.6 per cent per year in the 1980s and an average of 6.7 per cent in the five years following the acceleration of reforms in 1991.

The slowing pace of reforms in the mid-1990s was mirrored in a faltering growth rate in India (back down to 5.5 per cent per year from 1997–2002) while China continued to surge ahead with an annual GDP growth of 7–8 per cent during 1997–2001.

The consequences of this difference in growth rates are apparent from just a few figures. Over the past three decades, average annual per capita income growth was about 7 per cent in China compared to 2.5 per cent in India.

India's manufacturing production was slightly lower than that of China in the 1950s, but less than a quarter of China's manufacturing output in the late 1990s. Labour productivity, telephone density, and the use of electricity underwent similar divergences.

At the turn of the century, China's share in world trade (imports plus exports) was 3.3 per cent compared to India's 0.7 per cent. China received eighteen times the FDI India did.

A more discerning analysis of the historical record would, however, ameliorate this sharp contrast. Even while India's growth rates may have lagged behind China's, important progress was made in laying the foundations for sustained growth in the future. Food security was achieved through the Green Revolution. Capital-intensive industries were set up. Some of India's world-acclaimed centres of educational excellence such as the IITs, were also founded in the 1950s and 1960s.

And what of the future? As Edmund Burke once said, 'You can never plan the future by the past.' The question, 'Will China or India become Asia's economic power?' is essentially speculative. The answer depends on the future growth trajectories of the region's two largest economies.

I would argue that India has several advantages. China's growth remains higher than India's: official estimates place it at 9 per cent this year, though unofficial estimates are as high as 11–12 per cent.

These kinds of growth rates, coupled with investment patterns, are impressive, though some observers have raised the possibility of overheating.

Industrial production had risen by 17 per cent over the previous year as of October. And in the same month, investment was 32 per cent higher than in the previous year, despite signs of overinvestment in sectors such as cars, construction and coastal property.

A recent article in the *Asia Times* alludes to fears of a real estate bubble. Strong capital inflows and a fixed exchange rate have contributed to a growing money supply, and expectations of a coming revaluation of the yuan may have attracted speculative investment flows.

Inflation rates of 3 per cent in the year up to November 2003 are low by international standards, but the highest since April 1997.

India, however, has clearly reached the critical mass to achieve a quantum shift in its future growth trajectory. Nearly all indicators of development in India are trending positively—poverty incidence and infant mortality continue to fall while literacy rates, school enrolment, life expectancy and access to electricity and sanitation infrastructure are rising.

The growth rate has recently picked up, particularly in industry and services. The World Bank predicted a growth rate of 7 per cent over the 2003–04 fiscal year, but this figure may be too low given that growth in the second quarter of this fiscal year has been 8.2 per cent.

Four unique features of the Indian economy will support growth in the coming years. First, the advantages of an unusual demographic profile: India will have one of the youngest populations of the world, augmenting its workforce relative to other nations as well as providing a large base of workers freshly trained in the use of the latest technologies.

Second, there will be an acceleration of consumption. Thirty to forty million people are joining the middle class every year in India, representing a large and growing incremental increase in consumption spending. Improving infrastructure has also brought rural areas into the market and increased consumption spending from this source.

Third, India's growing knowledge reservoir and its already comparatively highly educated workforce and demonstrated capacity in biotech and software will contribute to growth.

Finally, growth in India will be augmented by rapid productivity increases. Given the recent technological improvements and the favourable 'incremental capital output ratio', modest investments of capital will lead to significant increases in productivity.

Both countries face important challenges, but I would argue that India's decades of practice with multiparty democracy is an advantage in terms of its ability to carry out the essential reforms—both political and economic—to sustain high rates of growth in the future.

Postscript

Since then India has experienced unprecedented growth buoyancy, continued GDP growth of over 9 per cent during the last three years with the manufacturing and services sectors remaining on a high growth curve. This augurs well for the achievements of the daunting targets contained in the recently adopted Approach Paper for the Eleventh Plan. The tardy growth in agriculture remains worrisome and it is sought to be addressed in the new initiatives unveiled in the 2007 budget. Similarly, improving the skill base by significantly enhancing outlays on education with particular emphasis on additional and restructuring of vocational training centres particularly ITIs in states is an important step forward. While the medium-term outlook for the Indian economy continues to be optimistic, a great deal depends on implementation, particularly in quickly improving the cost and quality of infrastructure. Getting a firm grip on the power sector remains a problem. The India story is the current fashion and policy makers need to be mindful for ensuring that action matches the rhetoric.

23 January 2004

11

India–China, the Great Asian Joint Venture (Part 2 of Two Part Series)

India's primary tasks are to address rising budget deficits and pare down continuing constraints on the market economy. Total public debt (including state-owned enterprises) stood at 95 per cent of the GDP as of March 2003 and primary deficits were over 3 per cent of the GDP.

The Tenth Plan target of increasing tax revenues to 10.3 per cent of the GDP by 2006–07 must be actively pursued. Attention must be paid to reducing agricultural and power sector subsidies that drain state and federal budgets.

The new federal Fiscal Responsibility and Budget Management Bill, as well as the matching state-level legislation, is an important step in the direction of fiscal discipline. This trend must be continued.

With regard to removing the key constraints on the Indian economy, several bottlenecks have been identified, both by external observers and in government reports. Among the most important challenges are to complete infrastructure reforms, dismantle remaining trade barriers, both internal and external, introduce flexibility in labour laws and complete tax reforms through the early introduction of a value-added system of taxation.

Future growth also depends on further financial liberalization, streamlining of industrial policy and the reduction of distortionary subsidies in the agriculture. The continued reforms carried out by this government are laying the macro-policy foundations for further growth. But it is important this 'reform accelerator' continues.

China, like India, faces growing fiscal deficit. At 5.3 per cent of the GDP this year, according to the IMF, it is lower than India's, but similar in that a large part is due to sub-national overspending. China also has the task of evolving an independent private sector, even as it faces the inevitable transition to a more open polity.

The past few decades of growth have been built on a hybrid economic structure of partnerships between the government and private enterprise. While this has been quite successful in the past and state-owned enterprises' (SOEs') production steadily rose over the past decades—output increased thirteen-fold from 1978 to 1997—the state-led model has inevitable limitations.

Enterprises involving the private sector now account for much of China's growth. This growth of the private sector raises the important challenge of improving corporate governance and regulation. China also faces the political challenge of restructuring the extensive network of less efficient SOEs, many of which currently provide social safety nets for workers.

China's deepening reforms in the financial sector are also essential to its sustained growth. The financial sector, the key to efficient capital allocation, is currently underdeveloped. Many private businesses, especially the potentially dynamic small and medium enterprises, are forced to resort to high-interest loans from the black market.

They have difficulty obtaining credit from the largely state-owned banks.

Transaction cost barriers to stock listings are too high for all but the largest enterprises.

The financial system is also burdened by an accumulation of bad loans. This will need to be resolved before the planned privatization in the financial sector.

India's long history of democracy will be an important advantage in the coming decades. Politically sensitive distributional questions have no doubt held India back from some earlier reforms, keeping in place inefficient industrial policies—reservation of the small-scale sector the Sick Companies Act—and other areas.

But the advantage of moving slowly has been to build consensus among stakeholders. India has spent many decades learning how to function as a society where power is not centralized, where there are many voices and conflicting interests are handled in a spirit of negotiation and consensus building.

The politico-economic foundations for the kinds of reforms mentioned above are firmly in place in India. We have strong support for the current reform-minded government and a growing middle class anxious for change that brings further opportunities.

The recent elections in several states demonstrated the growing importance of economic issues in the electoral psyche of the people. In this sense, the upcoming general election is more than ever before likely to be a referendum on this government's development policies—maintaining high growth rates, continuing reform initiatives and creating gainful employment opportunities.

China, on the other hand, faces questions about distribution that are augmented by its economic transition, without the same kind of experience with building consensus as India has developed.

The ongoing economic transition has created new political tensions—both in the form of newly economically empowered groups in society as well as unrest over the dismantling of SOEs. The process of integrating the much poorer, slower-growing inland provinces with their surging coastal counterparts also requires sensitive handling of issues such as labour migration.

Managing these kinds of transitions can be taxing. Fortunately, the Chinese leadership has shown sagacity and practical wisdom.

The answer to the question 'Will India or China become Asia's economic power?' is, however, not clear. But the question itself is somewhat limited.

Both countries are likely to play a significant role in the region. There will be inevitable competition. Both will vie for FDI, outsourcing jobs, market share in exports of manufacturing and services and the supply of skilled workers to the global labour force.

More important are the complementarities. There are already numerous opportunities for productive partnerships between Indian software and Chinese hardware, Indian R&D and Chinese manufacturing.

India–China trade is likely to be a dynamic regional source of growth, as both are large, fast-growing markets. This flow of goods and services will increase even more rapidly with concerted efforts at deeper integration or harmonization of standards, streamlining of customs processes, etc. Bilateral investment, similarly, will augment regional growth.

The greatest complementarity, however, is potential for learning from each other's experiences in the transition from state-led economies to the ever more open markets of today and tomorrow. As an old Hindu saying goes, 'There is nothing noble in being superior to someone else. The true nobility is being superior to your previous self.'

24 January 2004

12

The Future: Productivity and Sustainability

The Stanford conference on 'Challenges of Economic Policy Reform in Asia' which concluded on 3 June 2006 debated a variety of issues that concern Asia's future. One that affects India and China in particular—fiscal federalism—was the subject of one of my earlier essays. Two other areas that generated vigorous discussion were the comparison of productivity in India and China as well as energy, environment and sustainable development.

On productivity trends, the main issue was why total factor productivity in China has accelerated far more than in India. The broad conclusions converged on two factors: barriers to technology diffusion and misallocation of resources across firms. Total factor productivity could be doubled if capital and labour were allocated efficiently and bigger plants were allowed to expand. Medium-sized plants could also become more efficient. What is the key policy to enable diffusion of technology and improved resource allocation? Flexible labour policies and provisions for quicker entry and exit for firms. This will not only permit optimal technology use but also enable growth in a wider variety of geographic locations. Other policy priorities to address included minimizing financial distortions, reducing disproportionate taxes (based on equity considerations) on efficient firms, and scaling back specific policies which limit the size of firms (such as reservations for small-scale industries). All of these inhibit prospects for improving technology.

Whatever the route, India must improve total factor productivity, or its incremental capital–output ratio (ICOR), to realize the somewhat daunting growth targets contemplated for the Eleventh Five Year Plan. Simply increasing savings and investment will not be sufficient. The ICOR rates in India have barely moved over the past years. This is an area where the returns from some policy changes will have greater and faster impact on growth than efforts in other directions.

Also on the topic of technology, it was noted that while India is moving towards increased focus on research and development, there were still substantial barriers to fomenting and disseminating innovation. The recent passage of legislation protecting intellectual property rights was a step in the positive direction, but remains to be fully tested. In the medium term, however, protection of both technology transferred as well as the domestic companies' advances will contribute to innovation that is inspired by, and uniquely suited to, advancing India's economic growth. The framework for the financial sector reform to encourage financing of such innovation was a more complicated question. Here, the expertise of some of Silicon Valley's venture capital community was brought to bear. The primary focus should be on improving the legal basis to support the often complex contracts between investors and start-up companies.

Another interesting issue was the model and simulations in a paper titled 'China, the US and Sustainability: Perspectives Based on Comprehensive Wealth', by Nobel Laureate Kenneth Arrow, Partha Dasgupta, Lawrence Goulder, Kevin Mumford and Kirsten Oleson. Its analysis was designed to consider well-being and sustainability through comprehensive wealth accounting. This included valuing natural resources such as clean air and water as well as measuring human well-being.

Sustainability was being considered in a broader sense: in terms of the capacity to provide for the well-being of future generations. The principal indicator of a comprehensive measure of health was one that included both marketed and non-marketed assets. In the initial conclusions, and contrary to popular perception, in China, investments in reproducible capital (manufactured capital goods) contributed the most to increase in general wealth. Technology also played a significant role. China's depletion of natural resources has not yet had as big an impact on wealth as do the contributions from investment in reproducible and human capital.

The same is true of the US, where increases in human capital significantly outweigh the adverse wealth effects from resource depletion and higher oil prices.

Of course, many of these conclusions, they concede, depend greatly on the assumed shadow prices and the uncertainties surrounding technological change. Nonetheless, the assessment is contrary to the prevalent public perception that China's economic growth is resulting primarily from activities that damage air quality and water purity.

Population growth, productivity trends, and changing technology paradigms can dramatically alter these conclusions, however. Vinod Khosla's suggestions at the conference that technology will significantly alter the cost and availability of alternative fuels, and country energy models like those for India, call for a basic rethink of the models as well as great uncertainty. Also, one area which the analysis does not consider is that even while China's economic growth may be sustainable, its implications for the global economy needed closer examination. Pollutants know no boundaries.

The rich analysis, however, is well worth replicating for a large demographic entity like India, which will be a major energy guzzler and, by conventional wisdom, a big polluter with similar consequences. Certainly, while it is not easy to replicate this analysis, leaving out India would render this study incomplete. Uncertainties aside, however, energy, its security, its sustainable use, and the quest for alternative affordable energy forms to enhance productivity sustainably for the long run are at the heart of current geopolitics. In focusing on these issues, the Stanford conference has made a worthwhile contribution.

11 June 2006

III

GLOBAL MIGRATION

13

Coming Home to the Village

This year's Pravasi Bhartiya Diwas concluded about a week ago. The prime minister outlined the broad agenda to engage Non-Resident Indians (NRIs) by including economic, financial, intellectual and emotional participation. The finance minister is separately contemplating a Special Purpose Vehicle for an infrastructure fund that will be mutually beneficial, yielding both high returns and partly meeting our infrastructure financing needs.

Traditionally, NRIs have been a complaining—if not a demanding—lot. This has now changed greatly in at least two ways.

First, the new growth momentum and opportunities in India give them enough scope to participate in the development process. Second, both in the US and Europe, their new affluence and prosperity have made them valued partners and their contribution is being increasingly recognized. This new confidence, coupled with financial muscle, has made them a relevant player in political decision making. The significant contribution of the Indo-American community in galvanizing support for the enactment of the recent legislation on civil nuclear energy is a case in point.

While engagement at the national level will remain significant, a large number of non-residents relate more easily to their states of origin—their village, district, schools and colleges in which they spent their initial years. There are others who relate to the places from which their ancestors migrated, and generally there is a desire to make a contribution, to renew their bond, or to pay back in some form or the other.

Nostalgia and a search for identity are important drivers, and state-level engagement of NRIs will always remain meaningful. The initiatives of Andhra Pradesh, Gujarat and Maharashtra to engage NRIs at the state level have proved quite purposeful.

Bihar, which has a significant and flourishing non-resident community in the US and the UK, not to speak of Mauritius and the Caribbean, had so far lagged behind. From this point of view, the Global Meet for a Resurgent Bihar held in Patna this week marks a new beginning. President A.P.J. Abdul Kalam, while inaugurating the conference, dwelt on the multiple opportunities that Bihar has to offer.

The participation of Meghnad Desai, C. Rangarajan, Kirit Parikh, Y.C. Deveshwar and other representatives of international institutions and the state bureaucracy lent content and credence to the deliberations on the 'New challenges and opportunities for Bihar's development.' Alakh Sharma, director, Institute for Human Development, coordinated the meet and acted imaginatively in securing the participation of large number of non-resident Biharis in prominent positions—an impressive list that shows that while Biharis are doing well everywhere, Bihar languishes.

Micro-level efforts to engage non-residents may not garner significant financial resources but will certainly reinforce emotional ties. Most non-residents are hesitant to make contributions to any omnibus fund lest its identity gets lost and the money goes into something they don't particularly care about. That is why concepts like contribution to a Shiksha Kosh carried little attraction. Sometimes policies make this difficult. We need to devise guidelines that will facilitate their engagement, like:

- The creation of a financial corpus or a special development bond for a project that gives them satisfaction. This would also be useful to those who want to make a general contribution.
- Allowing schools in village or district and primary health centres to accept contributions and give suitable recognition.

- Allowing infrastructure investment at village or district level, perhaps by creating a single-window system for such contributions.
- Setting up foundations or trusts (as some states have done) facilitating continuous interaction with NRIs.
- Remittances, through inter-state and inter-country transfers, constitute a growing and substantial financial flow. While these are private funds designed to raise consumption and support expenditure in the housing and social sector, our ability to catalyse them in capital-creating assets remains a challenge.

Micro-engagement of NRIs is the way forward.

21 January 2007

14

The Dynamics of Managing Migration

A recent seminar on globalization organized by the National Council for Applied Economic Research (NCAER) reopened the controversies surrounding this subject. Needless to say, while globalization means different things to different people, a much closer economic interdependence of countries is a historical reality. Optimizing multiple opportunities even while mitigating risks is in everybody's interest. There is no fixed policy paradigm that addresses the concerns fully.

The prime minister, however, while dealing with the various aspects of globalization referred to Fukuyama's evocative concept of a borderless world, even while the focus of globalization has so far been on the movement of goods, capital and, largely, financial and logistical services. There is no framework for dealing with movement of people. He lamented that 'little attention has been paid to the economics and politics of managing migration in the uncertain world that we live in.'

The prime minister has, correctly, spotted a grave weakness in the area of international policy. The inability to evolve a coherent framework for managing migration has received international attention but has eluded consensus.

I served as a member of the Global Commission on International Migration, whose report inter alia formed the basis of the recently concluded United Nations high-level dialogue on international migration. Regrettably, while all the right things were said, the conclusion of that dialogue is colourless and fails to mainstream the key policy issues. This is another area where Jagdish Bhagwati has done some pioneering work.

In a holistic sense, there are at least five core issues. First, the need for a cohesive national policy. A country like India, which is a recipient of the largest number of irregular migrants (the legality of migration is always a debatable issue), is also the country of origin for a vast number of men and women of varied skills seeking a better quality of life elsewhere.

This duality of challenge is not easy to harmonize. Migration issues in India are still scattered across a number of ministries. The home ministry and the intelligence organizations are primarily concerned with enforcement and management of the border. The ministry of overseas Indian affairs now also has the office of the Protectors of the Immigrants. The ministry of external affairs is concerned with compliance to international conventions and treaties.

But who is concerned with skill inculcation, training and harmonizing demand and supply of talent, which enable global needs to be met without the adverse consequences of brain drain?

Those seeking immigration represent a broad spectrum—from unskilled labour to sophisticated software engineers, paramedics or even merchant bankers. Illustratively, in view of the huge shortage of paramedics in the United States, is it adequate that we leave to market forces the creation adequate nursing training institutes, which can combine a mutuality of benefits of meeting our needs and mitigating shortages experienced by others?

The fact remains that India does not have a migration policy. We need one. We also need a nodal entity (say, a ministry of migration and overseas Indians) which can coordinate a more cohesive approach.

Second, international migration is riddled with prejudices. The Europeans, burdened with high rates of unemployment, dread the prospects of a huge immigrant influx, which exacerbates existing social tensions and religious divides. Everyone knows that the process of European integration has been stalled due to fears of migration.

Perhaps not all countries in Europe have managed their policies as sensibly as the United Kingdom. The United States, traditionally being a more open society, and notwithstanding the Mexican migrant pressure, has reinvigorated its social and economic ethos by constantly inducting talent from the rest of the world. Perhaps, as the European economy gathers momentum and employment rates, particularly in France, significantly decline, a more rational view on migration might emerge.

Third, migration is a classic case of promoting sensible public–private partnership. Corporates do plan for their manpower and skill requirements, but fragmented action misses the big picture. There is no integrated plan, based on inter-corporate needs on projected skill requirements.

Only this can enable investment in human resource development to be made in a manner which can optimize the benefits of immigration. Mainstreaming emerging corporate needs into the national planning process is central to managing immigration in a non-contentious way. A global action plan on skill requirement and skill inculcation in which corporates are important players is an inescapable need of our time.

Finally, fragmentation of responsibilities on treaties and conventions, with many governments and international bodies, creates serious coordination problems.

The high-level dialogue held in September was designed to address these concerns. But even while recognizing the problem, it has finally decided to create a 'Global Forum' as a voluntary body, whose first meeting is to be hosted by Belgium in 2007.

I guess they will only repeat what has been repeated many times. Even while political will may be shy in accepting a 'borderless world', the logic of economic international dependence compels us to view migration far more innovatively than in the past.

Given the prime minister's concern, India can play a leadership role. The present international dialogue needs to be invigorated. Managing the dynamics of migration remains both complex and contentious. However, not doing so will prove very costly.

24 December 2006

15

A Moving Mantra

The Tenth Annual Wharton India Economic Forum held last week attracted speakers from varied disciplines and the private sector. The Wharton Global Business Forum, the overarching body behind the India Economic Forum, has annual interactions on Africa, Europe, Latin America, India and Asia, with the Asian one being devoted substantially to China, Japan and ASEAN countries. The organizational initiative rests with students; faculty members give a helping hand and the prestige of the Wharton Business School helps entice high-quality speakers.

Aditya Parekh's meticulous planning contributed to making the event a great success.

I found Wharton a mini-India: the highest percentage of students, both undergraduate and masters, come from India. The India session, with over 300 student participants in addition to alumni members and others interested in the programme, filled the large ballroom of the Hyatt. The room could well have been mistaken for the Crystal Room of the Taj Hotel in Mumbai. Indians such as Vice-Dean Anjani Jain and Jitendra Singh among the senior academic professors have served with distinction for over two decades. This, coupled with the presence of a large number of Indians who have received awards or the Director's Medal, added to the dominant Indian flavour.

This year, the broad theme of the India event was on India's mantra for success, interpreting success to mean India 'achieving its potential both in terms of economic and social development'. Panel sessions on 'Fostering Entrepreneurship', 'Investing in India', 'Emerging Company Profiles', 'Shaping India's Grassroots', 'Made in India', culminated in an overarching discussion of 'Government Policy: A Catalyst or a Barrier?' Speakers included Ahmass Fakahany, vice chairman and chief administrative officer, Merrill Lynch; Charles Kaye, co-president, Warburg Pincus; Sam Pitroda; Deepak Parekh; Swaminathan Aiyer; and myself. There were others who had success stories and anecdotal examples, like Avnish Bajaj, chairman, eBay, India; Vinod Ganjoor, chairman, Eurindia, not to mention a very effective intervention by Sonal Shah, founder of Indicorps and vice-president, Goldman Sachs and Company.

One overall impression which I have is that almost every student is keen to return to India. They do not necessarily seek to join his or her family business, but to do something different and creative, and to give back to the society which has enabled them to achieve these high skills. Anand Piramal, instead of returning to his father's business, has set up an organization called DIYA to rekindle entrepreneurship in Jhunjhunu, a poor district in Rajasthan. Sonal Jain has set up a microfinance organization from her savings. Several others want to engage in improving primary education in poorly attended schools. Many were keen on environmental improvement, particularly reducing urban pollution and encouraging more efficient energy management. Obviously, India is seen not only as a huge opportunity, but has kindled a sense of new patriotism, fostered by a climate which is amiable to change and improvement.

The question that I kept asking myself is, 'While the talented young Indians at Wharton are raring to go forward, is India doing enough to make the best use of their talent and motivation?' It is here that the issue of government as a catalyst or a barrier has great significance. While India is changing and regulations are being simplified, clearly, a lot more needs to be done, and quickly enough if the new fire ignited in these young minds is to be kept ablaze. Some of these issues, not surprisingly, centre around the well-known themes of how to improve governance, get better quality people into state legislatures and parliament, how to get the younger generation motivated to take part in political activity which can have a multiplier effect on changing the political scenario. Quite a few students were keen to create an organization like the American Generation Engage, which was set up by Adrian and Devon Talbott.

The second issue is how to motivate the lagging states, where a mindset change is not evident, to follow the more progressive states and reduce state-level barriers including multiplicity of permissions to do things which contribute to the common good and reduce corruption. Reducing corruption cannot be sustained without electoral changes and building incentive structures around political necessities to make these more transparent. These changes are needed to avoid dampening the energy of the young. The judicial process, while fair, is onerous and time-consuming.

It requires fundamental changes in reducing the burden of pendency.

Incidentally, the Whartonites were aware that the government was a principal litigant adding to case pendencies. Given the cumbersome nature of India's legislation, individual departments and offices mechanically pursue all layers of the appellate process to justify their innocence. Firewalling administrative institutions from excessive politicization should be pursued but in the end would need governance, political and electoral changes. While the government must not micromanage young people's aspirations, it certainly has the obligation to facilitate and to create an enabling environment in which the latent energies of the young can be put to best use.

The fervour and the commitment of the young Indians at Wharton were certainly moving. Will India move fast enough to harness their energies and in some modest way support their lofty dreams to realize India's mantra for success?

27 November 2005

16

Multiple Challenges of Global Migration

New York: Four days ago, the report of the Global Commission on International Migration (GCIM) titled 'Migration in an Interconnected World: New Directions for Action' was presented to UN Secretary General Kofi Annan. This Commission, of which I am a member, was constituted in 2003 as an independent body to 'analyse the gaps in current policy approaches to migration; and make recommendations to the Secretary General and others'. Over the last two years, the Commission held six regional hearings in the Asia Pacific, the Mediterranean, the Middle East, Europe, Africa, the Americas, and considered the views of a wide cross-section of society—government, trade unions, migrant organizations, academia, corporate management and civil society.

Migration is an inevitable facet of globalization. As new technologies enable a seamless transfer of capital, goods, services, information and knowledge, freer movement of people is now a reality. Consider the following facts:

- There are over 200 million international migrants in 2005, a number which has increased rapidly from eighty-two million in 1972 and 125 million in 2000.
- Almost half of the world's international migrants are women and there are more female than male migrants in Asia, the Caribbean and Europe.
- There are sixty-six million migrants in Europe accounting for 8

per cent of Europe's population, fifty million in Asia and just forty million in North America. The USA is the host country for thirty-five million constituting 20 per cent of the world's migrants followed by Russia with just over thirteen million.
- Among the countries of origin, the Chinese diaspora has over thirty-five million people followed by India with twenty million and Philippines with seven million.
- Interestingly, while 60 per cent of the world's migrants live in developed countries, a sizeable 40 per cent reside in the developing countries.

The factors which have contributed to a dramatic increase in migration include:

The demographic differential: Many of the more prosperous nations have a fertility ratio significantly below the replacement rate of 2.1 per cent per woman. Their population is becoming smaller and older, a scenario which threatens their ability to sustain current levels of economic growth, pension and social security system.

According to the UN Population Division, the estimated fertility rates for the period 2000–05 range from 1.4 in Europe, 2.5 in Latin America and a high of 5.4 in sub-Saharan Africa. The World Bank estimates that the global labour force in the period 2000–10 will have an annual increase of forty million per year; thirty-eight million will come from developing countries and only two million from high-income countries.

Wage disparities: 45.7 per cent of people earn less than $1 per day in sub-Saharan Africa, 14.4 per cent in South Asia and 10 per cent in Latin America.

Unemployment rates: At 7.22 per cent in the Middle East and North Africa, 11 per cent in sub-Saharan Africa and 6.5 per cent in the industrialized countries.

Educational differentials: Only 58 per cent women and 68 per cent men are literate in low-income countries with almost 100 per cent literacy in the advanced countries.

Finally, democracy and quality of governance: The Commission has concluded that 'by migrating, people who are living in disturbed economic and political circumstances are able to insure themselves and their families against market uncertainties, political crises, armed conflicts and other risks'.

The issue of migrants' contribution to host countries is beginning to secure recognition. They are making a significant contribution in mitigating labour shortages, and maintaining production at competitive costs obviating the need for outsourcing. Their supply chain now extends from mechanical functions to high-value-added activity, sustaining the knowledge economy in innovation-driven societies.

The remittances that the migrants send home has become increasingly significant with formal transfers in 2004 exceeding $150 billion with an estimated $300 billion additional transfer sent informally. This is a multiple of the Official Development Assistance and second only to Foreign Direct Investment. However 60 per cent of the remittances are sent to developing countries with Mexico receiving sixteen billion dollars per year followed by India at around eleven billion dollars and the Philippines at 8.5 billion dollars.

While the developmental impact of remittance is obvious there are other contentious issues on migration, particularly irregular migration, refugees and asylum seekers. An estimated 2.5 to four million migrants cross the international borders without authorization each year and at least five million of Europe's fifty-six million migrants are irregular while the number in the US is double. India has over twenty million migrants with irregular status while 50 per cent of the Mexican-born population in the US in 2000 had an irregular status.

There is no doubt that migration will continue to rise rapidly in the decades ahead. The multifaceted challenge which this creates needs a coherent international response.

How should the world respond to a freer interchange of people? How can the mutuality of benefit be forged between countries of origin and countries of destination?

9 October 2005

17

Brain Gain Vs Brain Drain

The issue of relationship between migration and development has multiple dimensions which, inter alia, include methodological ambiguities in establishing a firm relationship between migration and development. The asymmetric distribution of resources, in which one country experiences 'brain drain' and the other 'brain gain', has generated considerable literature. One issue that is clear, however, is that financial flows (on which data are relatively good) between countries are an important part of this relationship. Yet there is substantial room for policy change to increase the benefits from these flows.

Total remittances and other current transfers received by developing countries in 2001 exceed $99 billion, of which remittances constitute $73 billion, which is 250 times the percentage of all Official Development Assistance (ODA) flows and indeed represent 42 per cent of all FDI. According to the IMF Balance of Payments Yearbook, as reproduced in the article 'Workers' Remittances' by Dilip Ratha, India in 2001 received over $10 billion by way of workers' remittances followed closely by Mexico. The top twenty countries from where remittances were sourced has the USA heading the list with over $28.4 billion, followed by Saudi Arabia at $15.1 billion.

The multiplier benefits of remittance incomes are particularly significant in relation to low-income countries and middle-income countries where, for instance, in the case of Tongo, they constitute 37 per cent of the GDP as against 8 per cent in the case of the Philippines and much lower percentage in other more advanced developing countries. While in the lower-income countries, they are a direct source in sustenance of consumption and production patterns, in others, they constitute a source of capital, technology and investment which have a higher sustainable impact on medium-term growth trends. Several developing countries are pursuing deliberate incentive policies to encourage the utilization of remittances for investment expansion rather than meet current consumption needs, but in most cases, while the balance may change, they represent a blend of both consumption and investment.

There are, however, several complex issues relating to the interrelationship between development and remittances which still require a more transparent regime.

Contrary to popular belief, the push for migration emanates not from the poorest but from the better-off sections of the population segment. Indeed, it is only the somewhat better off, looking for further improvement in the quality of life, who can afford to bear the cost and time of the tedious procedures connected with migration.

In this sense, migration patterns could further exacerbate growing regional inequalities. This pattern is also true of migration within countries and regions where the very poor get left behind while it is the somewhat better off who are willing to encounter risks and costs associated with migratory patterns.

Historical time series data also suggest that remittances, while less volatile and sensitive to business-cycle fluctuations than other forms of capital flows, are still highly susceptible to the overall macroeconomic policies being pursued by recipient nations.

Data available with international institutions reveal that the cost of remittance transfers is steep and the cost of intermediated fund transfers from overseas workers to families unacceptably high. O'Neil (2003) reports that sending small amounts of money ($200) from the US to other countries can cost as much as 13–16 per cent in some ethnic exchange houses and money-sending services. These costs impose a large additional tax on workers' earnings. Some authors estimated that the remitter collected about $12 billion in fees in 2001.

Given the impact of the new money laundering legislation coupled with implications of terrorism on unofficial channels of transfer, many banks are now either opening or diversifying banking channels or creating special purpose vehicles to facilitate such remittances which may in turn lower these fees. The international community, recognizing that such remittances are only likely to increase, should foster public–private partnership in creating institutions or arrangements which facilitate such flows at more acceptable costs.

The ongoing controversy of brain gain versus brain drain must be seen in the broader context that while fiscal losses may have been caused due to worker migration and the structure of taxation arrangements, what is sent back by way of remittance far exceeds what would have been realized by the tax authorities for meeting public expenditure. For example, in the article by Desai and Kapoor, it has been estimated that the end fiscal loss associated with Indian immigration to the USA may be in the region of 0.24 per cent to 0.58 per cent of the Indian GDP in 2001 but remittances amounted to at least 2.1 per cent of the GDP during the same fiscal year.

Looking at the problem from this point of view would, in my view, be somewhat myopic. Developing countries subsidize the education process through institutional arrangements and public expenditure through investment in HRD, which enable a significant proportion of migrants to seek gainful high-value employment opportunities in the country of their work.

The contribution to value and wealth made by such highly skilled and knowledge-based migrants is quite significant in many economies and the total value of remittance made to the country of their origin represents only a small fragment of the value added in their country of work. It would be reasonable to consider some form of tax sharing to compensate the sending countries more equitably for their contribution to human capital development. Some of these thoughts have also been raised by Jagdish Bhagwati in 'Borders beyond Control' (2003), a persuasive case for taxation arrangements, which in some way enables a more appropriate apportioning of the gains and contributions made by such migrants between their country of origin and their country of work.

These issues are, however, more complex and may need innovative arrangements to compensate developing countries and permit adequate resources in human development skills for global gains.

Need for a New Normative Approach

There is no doubt that the scale of migration over the next ten to fifteen years will only increase. Conservative estimates suggest that over 100 million new people are likely to seek a better quality of life. As inter- and intra-regional disparities become more accentuated and are coupled with a skewed demographic profile, these numbers will assume unimaginable proportions. Moral issues of whether there should be an international framework that revisits the traditional definition of sovereign nations or redefines nationalism in the revised context require much greater international debate and consensus.

Economic compulsion will force nations to increasingly move away from sovereign predilections on migration-based issues to productivity and efficiency-based predilections designed to maximize economic benefit. The ongoing debate on outsourcing is one facet of the problem. If large-scale movement of people is less acceptable both due to economic and moral reasons, the fragmentation of economic activity into most efficient divisible entities may be a more acceptable response.

In the short term, this would of course increase the pressure to reconcile sustainable higher rates of growth, which are driven by productivity enhancement with the creation of gainful employment opportunities. In the medium term, however, if economic activity is to be undertaken in the primary country of origin, there is no escape from accepting to 'manage migration' on an unprecedented scale.

International conventions, rules and regulations, which are fragmentary and implementation of and which are spread over a number of organizations, need to be reconsidered. A new normative approach which fills existing gaps or the creation of a truly cohesive multilateral framework which holistically addresses these emerging issues would be an appropriate response. Whatever the outcome, one conclusion is clear—demography and migration will be the most critical challenges which the coming decade must address. The sooner the debate generates and brings out the interrelated issues, the better it would augur for a more stable and prosperous world.

Demographic profiles, complex issues concerning the migrants themselves, and the interrelationship between migration and development including choice patterns between movement of men or the disaggregating of economic activity all require sensitive and innovative approaches.

The economic and moral issues in the allocation of resources between the old and the young go beyond the somewhat simplistic definition of Albert Camus, who had said that 'to grow old is to move from passion to compassion'. In fact, the dilemma was more appropriately reconciled by Mahatma Gandhi when he explained that 'it is nonsense for you to talk of old age so long as you outrun young men in the race for service and in the midst of anxious times fill rooms with your laughter and inspire youth with hope when they are on the brink of despair'.

26 April 2004

IV

MULTILATERAL RELATIONS

18

A New Year beyond Resolutions

We usher in the new year with a nominal one-second adjustment to compensate for the wobbly planet. Unfortunately, a much deeper correction is necessary to compensate for our wobbly policies. Will 2006 usher in a healthier and happier world than the one we have left behind last year? To make the world a better place, we need a more enduring response to some key concerns:

- First, the economic and social consequences of ageing. The crisis of ageing in mature societies, simultaneously with the problems of the young in the developing world, needs a coherent response. Japan, Europe and the USA face a decline in fertility rates with an increased ratio of the old to the young, and with the growing problems of an inadequate workforce even compensating for productivity-enhancing advancements, a crumbling healthcare system with rising costs, declining consumption and savings at the same time for asymmetric reasons. Social security schemes are under increased strain which involves moral choices on intergenerational resource allocation. The comparatively young demography in Asia, particularly India and China, and large parts of Africa, have a different set of problems of skill inculcation with investment in human resource development and meaningful employment for new labour force entrants. Rising savings and a desire to improve the quality of life prompts migration within their country, their region or to the more developed countries.

The continuous relocation of economic activity, apart from technological limitations, may become cost inefficient. Accepting and integrating large migrations create serious problems of lifestyle and cultural imbalances, threatening the cohesiveness of societies. The implications of managing and preparing for an ageing world go far beyond the resolutions of either the First World Assembly on Ageing, Vienna, 1982 or the Second World Assembly, Madrid, 2002, namely to implement an integrated plan even while technology paradigms constantly alter choice patterns.

- Second, global warming, namely that while earth's temperature, with rapid global warming over the past thirty years, 'is now passing through a peak level of Holocene, a period of relatively stable climate that has existed for more than 10,000 years', any further warming by more than one degree Celsius will make the earth warmer than in a million years. This results in serious climatic change and environmental degradation which will unsettle civilization patterns and energy-driven economic activity. Drawing solace that in the planet's history these are reversible changes or that the data are either exaggerated or inconclusive detracts a resolute response to complex challenges. As Nikito Loquinine, the chairman of the World Commission on Protected Areas, says 'as glaciers recede and disappear, water will become scarce, droughts will increase and farm crops will fail. The ice on Africa's Mt Kilimanjaro is nearly gone, conflicts are inevitable, we cannot live without water; can hope that our children have some to drink.' While this may happen, large parts of the world in the interim may get submerged with rising sea levels; shrinking agriculture and changing habitation patterns will make readjustments more difficult and painful. An implementation plan must look beyond the resolutions of the Kyoto Protocol or the just-concluded meeting on climate change in Montreal.
- Third, connected with the above, is the need for an efficient energy policy which decreases dependence both on fossil fuel and energy intensity to sustain the current lifestyle. Drawing comfort from the fact that there are vast, unexplored, untapped sources of oil and gas in more environmentally hazardous areas, postpone

massive investments in alternative fuels and alternative ways of economic production. Can we lead an acceptably healthy, long life which does not need so much energy? Inefficient energy pricing and distortionary cross-subsidy structures have untenable consequences. Expecting the highest wasters to economize, optimize and seek alternatives may spare conflicts to secure energy at desired prices in a self defeating competetive race.

- Fourth, the number of people who will fail to achieve the minimum prescribed in Millennium Development Goals (MDGs) in terms of poverty, longevity and other key indicators in the Human Development Index remains alarming. Renewed interest in funnelling higher resources to Africa to improve healthcare and redress poverty needs remains well below the acceptable minimum. The diluted UN resolution on the achievement of the MDGs at the recent session of the UN General Assembly has some brave words with inadequate resource commitments. Further, there are unresolved problems of implementation and enhancing the reach and capability of multilateral financial institutions to meet their vastly enlarged obligations.

Raging ethnic conflicts, growing religious intolerance, vain attempts to replicate preferred political and economic institutions with an enhanced sense of insecurity are simultaneous consequences of decadent leisure societies existing alongside abject poverty. The numerous resolutions on human rights and humanitarian approaches on suffering adopted by various agencies of the United Nations appear grossly inadequate to arrest this new phase of intolerance.

Global commitment to address these challenges must go beyond resolutions. It must go beyond diplomatic skills in adopting finely balanced outcomes. One can be cynical that individual or national self-interest always overrides compassion and empathy is never deep enough to conquer detractions. Nonetheless, the new year must begin on a note of optimism. Can 2006 be somewhat different?

1 January 2006

19

Do Nations Have the Collective Guts to Look Global Risk in the Face?

In October 2006, I took part in the Evian XI Plenary 2006, held in Montreux, Switzerland, as a keynote speaker. The conference addressed the theme: 'The Grave Crisis of Globalization: How Can We Regenerate the Momentum?' The Evian Group, founded in 1995, is an international coalition of corporate, government and opinion leaders committed to 'fostering an open, inclusive, equitable and sustainable global market economy'. The plenary saw the participation of reputed academicians, successful new-generation entrepreneurs, policy makers and ambassadors to the WTO.

The failure of the Doha round (many view it as mere suspension, others as active suspension and a few as a creative pause) has reopened the issue of multilateral versus preferential trading agreements. There is no finality to the debate on whether preferential agreements are a stepping stone or a stumbling block to more generalized liberalization and the extent to which such suboptimal trading and economic activities generate vested interests.

The concerns were that many preferential agreements would somehow lock in trading patterns so that broader groups of countries could not form. They might have already specialized to cater to narrow groups, or they might develop complex administrative apparatuses to oversee preferential trade and be unwilling to open these up.

In practice, preferential trade agreements are on the rise. This is not necessarily sad, since the preferential agreements among smaller, possibly more similar, or more cooperative and mutually trusting groups of countries, may allow deeper integration and economic cooperation. But it does remain to be seen whether this results in a more fragmented global economy.

The question of global risk evoked a mixed response from all participants. These, as perceived by insurers, were per se not so contentious as forging a consensus for meaningful responses.

We generally accept the need to address climate chaos, radical poverty, organized crime, extremism in the form of terrorist activity, disruptive innovations (particularly in informatics, genetics, artificial intelligence and nanotechnology), and integration of financial capital markets testing our ingenuity in optimizing resource allocations. These have been discussed and analysed in many forums.

The one elusive question is their interrelationship, because, say, alleviation of extreme poverty may require development initiatives which significantly raise the utilization of fossil fuel energy, which could further exasperate climate chaos. The emerging innovations in genetic, informatics and nanotechnology could sharply raise longevity, creating a new demographic challenge even as differentials in ageing patterns need more imaginative immigration policies that are not disruptive to social cohesiveness. Contradiction in policies designed to address these risks entails prioritization and sequencing of action on which there are no easy answers.

Discussions on regenerating the faltering momentum of globalization exaggerate the consequences of the stalled Doha trade liberalization efforts. Globalization in a broader sense is not an event but a continuing process prompted by changing technology paradigms and the ability to disaggregate economic activity into micro but optimal divisible entities.

These, along with seamless transfer of technology, know-how and capital have imparted an irreversible momentum to the interdependence of economies. Nonetheless, the institutions for global governance remain outmoded and ill equipped to deal with these new challenges.

This is not a surprise. Why should we expect to see coöperation, goodwill and solidarity when we have no institutional or cultural basis for securing it? Economic historians and modern economists are reasonably clear that these institutions must provide a credible basis for cooperation in several spheres, particularly to sustain a functioning cooperative market, resolve disputes in a manner considered fair and equitable, set norms that spell out obligations in interactions between nations, secure mutually recognized property rights, redress the development deficit of the unfortunate members of our planet and create governance structures that address these challenges.

Unfortunately, few international organizations have the credibility to do so. These are frequently undercut by individual countries, their reforms are not radical enough and some of them have not restructured to mirror the new configurations of economic power.

Analysts generally agree that the current cycle of continuing global prosperity cannot last forever. While emerging opportunities look boundless, failure to address perceived risks can lead to large unintended consequences. Coherent action to address global risks cannot be left to crystal-gazing of insurance and re-insurance companies, which no doubt evaluate actuarial risks for 250 years. Collective political will remains elusive. So does our ability to manage global risks.

22 October 2006

20

The World Bank Needs India As Much As We Need It

Paul Wolfowitz, the tenth president of the World Bank, has just concluded his first visit to India in August 2005. Notwithstanding NGOs protesting against water privatization in Delhi, the visit was constructive and non-controversial. Contrast this with what one of his predecessors, Robert McNamara, encountered in 1968, described in I.G. Patel's *Glimpses of the Indian Economy*, when Left parties had vowed not to let him enter Calcutta, and ultimately, since Calcutta airport was surrounded on all sides by protesters, he had to be taken in a helicopter to the governor's residence.

It's a sign of changed times that the chief minister of the Left-ruled West Bengal is currently wooing investors in Singapore.

The fund-bank division of economic affairs had prepared well and Chidambaram struck the appropriate chord in seeking constructive partnership. The debate about additionality, namely three billion plus, is sterile; there is significant unutilized borrowing headroom. Successful projectization, high disbursement, counterpart funds and absorptive capacity are the real constraints.

Both the IMF and the World Bank originated in the aftermath of World War II as an outcome of the UN Monitoring and Finance Conference at Bretton Woods, New Hampshire, in July 1944 as part 'of the concerted effort to finance the reconstruction of Europe after the war and also save the world from future economic depression'.

The real name of the World Bank—The International Bank for Reconstruction and Development (IBRD)—explains its mission.

Curiously, Joseph Stiglitz, in his book, *Globalization and Its Discontents*, comments that 'development was added almost as an afterthought.' India was among seventeen original participants of the 1944 Bretton Woods conference and it was apparently the Indian delegation which suggested the name, IBRD! Over the years, the structure of the Bank has become more broad-based, encompassing five closely associated developed institutions—International Bank for Reconstruction and Development (IBRD), International Development Association (IDA), International Finance Corporation (IFC), Multilateral Investment Guarantee Agency (MIGA) and International Centre for Settlement of Investment Disputes (ICSID).

The birth of IDA in 1960 was recounted by I.G. Patel when an India-sponsored initiative for a Special UN Fund for Economic Development (SUNFED), making UN the pioneer in development assistance, resulted in the US 'accepting a lesser evil, namely, the International Development Association (IDA), under the World Bank'.

Till date, India has a cumulative borrowing of 64.6 billion dollars and a current portfolio of sixty-six projects with a commitment of 13.2 billion dollars with a planned average annual commitment of 3 billion dollars. The World Bank's country strategy for the four-year period—July 2004 to June 2008—envisages increasing the World Bank lending to India from 2 billion dollars to 3 billion dollars per annum. The current portfolio of the World Bank has a high concentration of 43 per cent in infrastructure and the balance in the social sector. The state sector loans cover Andhra Pradesh, Uttar Pradesh, Rajasthan, Madhya Pradesh and Karnataka.

India's relationship with the World Bank can be seen in three phases. In the first phase, as a source of project financing to support large capital expenditure at a time when access to external credit was limited. Bimal Jalan, in his book, *The Future of India*, explains how in the 1950s and early 1960s, the vast expansion of Indian public sector undertakings ('temples of modern India', in the words of Pt Nehru) and the balance of payment crisis in 1956 led to the creation of the Aid India Consortium in 1958 under the leadership of the World Bank to increase official and multilateral aid by industrial economies.

In Phase II, notwithstanding liberalization efforts, in the 1980s, our balance of payments remained fragile and an external crisis loomed large. The economic crisis in 1991 obliged us to seek World Bank resources along with the IMF facilities to finance critical imports and honour debt obligations. However, even during the 1980s, the line of distinction between the IMF and the World Bank had got increasingly blurred. Access to the Structural Adjustment Loan (SAL) of the Bank was contingent on a successful conclusion of an arrangement with the IMF and the other way round. Thus, between 1991 and 1993, access to these funds was contingent on significant changes covering trade, industrial regulation, banking and financial sector reform, apart from fiscal prudence to ensure macroeconomic stability.

In Phase III, beginning from the mid-1990s, the World Bank has become an active development partner and has even tried to mainstream policies in state governments with the national objectives. For central sector projects, its policy prescriptions have increasingly mirrored what we have ourselves adopted in the Ninth and Tenth Five Year Plans. They have increasingly realized the limitations of preconceived development paradigms in the so-called Washington Consensus, an expression used by John Williamson of the Institute of International Economics which is broadly a laundry list of the World Bank and the IMF-favoured approach on development.

So what does the World Bank now mean to India?

First, it continues to be a valuable source for long-term external credit at costs which are lower than domestic or external borrowings. These long-term assured flows are more efficient than alternative financing modes—suitable for infrastructure like roads, power, ports, airports, rural roads.

Second, given the high poverty ratio, we continue to be eligible for concessional financing even for the current fourteenth replenishment cycle, valuable for sustaining the social sector, particularly health, education, rural sanitation and can be blended with IBRD financing.

Third, given increased market deregulation, public–private partnership would need creative financial engineering. Several worthwhile projects may require government subsidy (popularly known as the viability gap) to secure financial closure; useful for the proposed Special Purpose Vehicle and Viability Gap financing.

Fourth, from the late 1990s, the Bank's engagement with state governments was concentrated on the better-performing states. The new policy of reaching out to the poor-performing states is an experiment whose outcome would be keenly watched.

Is the Bank imposing conditions which circumscribe our economic sovereignty?

This is a somewhat misunderstood concept. As a banker, prudential lending and long-term viability is a legitimate concern. As borrowers, we are free not to accept or re-negotiate terms. In the end, both the borrower and the lender need mutuality of comfort and benefit.

Success, they say, has a million followers while failure is a lonely furrow. India is a success story and the Bank among others would like to be seen as part of this success. We need not grudge it this comfort. In the fifty-seven years of interaction, our needs and their predilections have undergone tectonic shifts. There are not too many borrowers with large demands and a credible record. We need the Bank but the Bank needs us as much. That is why Wolfowitz's keenness in embracing us as equal partners reflects the prevalent perception.

28 August 2005

21

The Quest for 'Pahale India'

The twenty-first India Economic Summit of the World Economic Forum concluded on 29 November 2005. For Klaus Schwab, the founder-chairman, India has always remained a priority partner. Old India hands at the Forum like Colette Mathur painstakingly kept faith in India for over two decades believing that one day we will do the right things to make us a global power. That day could be round the corner. Not only has the Indian economy changed dramatically, becoming the current global flavour, but the openness with which we are willing to discuss the opportunities and constraints does constitute a mindset change.

An innovative feature this year was the town hall meeting in which participants voted and identified the factors which could collectively improve India's ranking in the Global Competitiveness Index. The voting outcome in the town hall meeting was compared with a fairly representative opinion poll conducted by NDTV.

Currently, India ranks fifty out of the total of 117 economies evaluated in 2005–06. Before the town hall meeting, there were interactive sessions on 'India and the World: Scenarios to 2025'. Three types of scenarios were considered, namely, the 'Bolly World', which has glitter 'with an illusion of success', 'Atakta Bharat'—getting stuck without direction, and 'Pahale Bharat'—meaning, India First, a virtuous circle where all things go right.

Broadly speaking, the outcome of both the scenario exercise and the global competitiveness exercise were quite similar. A very high percentage, 45 per cent in the town hall and 72 per cent in the NDTV poll considered it very important for India to become one of the ten best-performing economies in the world. On the factors which would help India achieve this were high-quality infrastructure: roads, ports, airports, water and power followed by effective government spending. On the sort of problems most likely to affect the future prosperity of individuals and families, the town hall audience gave high importance to infrastructure followed by minimizing corruption; whereas in the NDTV survey, it was enhanced access to Internet, telephone and increased tele-density. On the issues on which India's top companies should play a bigger role, it was infrastructure again, followed by reducing corruption. And finally, on the question of which problem the participants felt most confident that the government could solve within the next ten years, it was access to information technology followed by infrastructure. Surprisingly, a high 25 per cent felt that government could solve none of these.

On action points, a majority of the participants felt that the most efficient way on infrastructure would be to leverage private resources and capabilities through vastly improved regulatory mechanisms and create more credible models for public–private partnership. Even on improving tele-density in rural areas, the model of public–private partnership was the preferred course of action. On reducing corruption, the way forward was to streamline processes, reduce discretionary decision making and for corporates 'to remain united'. in making political contributions only in a transparent manner.

What surprises me is not the overwhelming consensus for improving infrastructure but inadequate concern for priority to governance reforms in general and electoral reform in particular which has eluded successive governments. While electoral outcomes have increasingly become development-centric even in a state like Bihar and with the symmetry between economic and social development being increasingly recognized, broad-based economic strategy needs the underpinning of governance reforms. Regrettably, the dominance of coalition politics limits flexibility and the absence of consensus between the two mainstream parties remains a serious impediment. For India to become one of the top ten competitive economies, there is a need for simultaneous action on multiple concerns. The new mantra of public–private partnership is not a substitute either for credible regulatory framework for which the current appetite is somewhat low.

Why has public–private partnership not taken off to a more credible start? In the case of power, multiple issues relating to tariff policy, open access, phasing out distortionary subsidies, completing distribution reforms, and accepting the culture for user charges remain debatable. Large private investments in power have yet to gather momentum. On improving rural tele-density, prevarication on the preferred model, minimizing service charges and subsidy through competitive bidding as well as the implementing mechanism along with inadequacy of resources remain a challenge. The Rural Roads Programme remains underfunded and depends on widely differing implementation quality between and across states. While the newly created special purpose vehicle on infrastructure and the viability gap fund would help in unbundling risks to achieve financial closure, its credible implementation is yet to begin. Improving the efficiency of public expenditure remains a complex issue and improving the quality of public services goes beyond the arithmetic of the outlay–outcome statement to include incentivizing and improving the efficiency of the field officials with greater financial delegation coupled with accountability.

Surprisingly, the exogenous variable, namely, continued global prosperity and peace in the subcontinent, was taken for granted. So was continued energy security and availability of fossil fuel energy at tolerable costs. The latter by no means can be assumed.

The recent summits notwithstanding, its overall optimism helps us prioritize our key concerns and more so the convergence in key areas necessitating simultaneous action on multiple fronts. This is easier said than done. So is the challenge to become a leading economic powerhouse to realize the quest of 'Pahale India'.

4 December 2005

22

What Gets Measured Gets Done

The Bretton Woods Institutions meet in Singapore for their annual meeting, seeking to reinvent their relevance. Unfortunately, excessive preoccupation with reassigning quotas detracts attention from a failure to redress the growing global structural imbalances which create uncertainty on the prospects of a soft landing.

Just prior to their meeting, the World Bank released a report titled 'Doing Business 2007—How to Reform', which compares regulations in 175 countries. This is the fourth in a series of annual reports investigating the regulations that enhance business activity and those which constrain them.

Despite our improved economic performance, we do not rank among the top reformers in 2005–06. In fact, our position in the table of rankings on 'the ease of doing business' only marginally improves from 138 in 2006 to 134 in 2007.

The methodology of assessment is based on ten evaluation parameters. On starting a business in terms of number of procedures, cost and time, we rank eighty-eighth. On the criteria of licensing requirements, particularly in the construction sector, we rank 155th, with twenty procedures to be followed and a time cost of 270 days! On the index of employing workers and the rigidity of working hours, we rank 112th. Not surprisingly, on the index of firing workers we rank 170th and the cost of severance stands at fifty-six weeks' salary.

On registration of property, we rank low at 110th, with a time of sixty-two days and a cost of 7.8 per cent of the property value and involving six procedures. On securing credits, we rank sixty-fifth, significantly better than other criteria and similarly on protection of investors at thirty-third. On paying taxes we rank 158th despite extensive tax reforms undertaken by us. On trading across borders we rank 139th, with the cost of imports at $1,244 per container, while cost of exports is $864 per container and time taken to export is twenty-seven days. On enforcement of contracts, we are a poor 173rd, with fifty-six procedures and 1,420 days. On business exit we rank 133rd, taking upto ten years and paying recovery rates at 13 cents per dollar.

There is a disclaimer in the report that the methodology employed has limitations. The indicators are used to analyse economic outcomes and identify what reforms have worked but macro indicators such as the strength of institutions have not been studied to make meaningful cross-country analyses.

The policy prescriptions suggested in the report are in themselves not startling. However, it is somewhat depressing that even after a decade of economic reforms, we rank so low as a country to do business in. Obviously, while others have changed, we have either not changed significantly enough or the changes made by others compel us to change faster.

On each of the ten indices, the policy prescriptions have some obvious lessons. For starting a business clearly most countries have adopted administrative reforms, namely, cutting unnecessary procedures, creating a one-stop shop for business registration, introducing standard applications and a single business identification number which can be utilized for multiple purposes. Not many states in India have adopted a single-window approach, and in spite of the many empowered committees, our record on this score remains a mixed one. While a personal account number (PAN) is available, the need to have a unique identification number which has multiple uses in accessing information and securing permissions is yet to be conceived.

On credit availability, our record is somewhat better but countries which have performed well have a vastly improved system of credit information registry and a diversified menu on assets, which can be used as collaterals for lending. In short, this recent report is a painful reminder that we still need to improve in several areas to create a competitive investment environment. We need to consider the comparative data on the ease of doing business with a view to determine the policy changes needed to improve our competitive performance.

The report concludes that in the end 'what gets measured gets done'. In our case measurements may be easy, but getting them done requires a combination of political will and administrative skills. Only time will tell if these can be combined to further improve international perception in making us a truly competitive investment destination.

17 September 2006

V

INFRASTRUCTURE

23

When Sacred Cows Block the Intersection

While much of the media and policy debate focuses on private infrastructure providers, most of India's roads, ports, airports, telephone connections, electricity and other infrastructure are provided by public sector companies or departments.

Their performance obviously has an enormous impact on the quality of infrastructure. Every rupee spent on obsolete equipment, or not spent on maintenance, means one more reason for complaint for customers. But it is not just customers that are affected; public sector performance affects private providers' services as well as the overall business climate for private entry. Public entities are customers, competitors, suppliers and carriers of private infrastructure services.

In telecom, private investors compete with public companies in all segments of the market. Service quality depends on interconnection with the public networks BSNL and MTNL, which provide most of the fixed-line service and a significant share of wireless services. Many—though not all—of the most congested interconnections are between BSNL and private companies.

Similarly, in the transport sector, private operators compete with public companies and rely on them as interconnected transport network and service providers. The public sector Indian Airlines still accounts for just over 21 per cent of domestic air travel, the second-largest market share among domestic airlines. Airlines land and take off at publicly owned and operated airports where runway traffic forces planes to burn costly time and fuel in circling.

Regulatory favouritism for public sector companies, real or perceived, has a deterrent effect on potential competitors in both sectors. Regulators' choices, whether in allocating lucrative air routes or scarce telecom spectrum, have the ability to dramatically shift companies' fortunes.

These public companies are the sacred cows in the middle of a busy intersection. They cannot be hurried or bothered but at the same time they are risky customers, unreliable carriers and threatening competitors that clog the flow.

What steps can be taken to clear the crossroads of these cows and improve public infrastructure provisions?

First, India must continue and accelerate the move towards more commercial practices. Competitively selected professional management, even through international recruitment, should become more common. International competitive bidding is as important for talent as for projects. Benchmarking between public enterprises and private competitors, as is proposed for public sector banks, is also important.

Listed public sector undertakings should also increase the proportion of independent directors (and thereby the potential expertise and oversight) to the Securities and Exchange Board of India (SEBI) standard of half. It is likely that this will require some reduction in the number of government appointees.

Second, the norms for public companies should be altered to remove procedural restrictions that both hamper performance and provide excuses for poor returns. The most commonly cited constraints or excuses are that public companies have to obey civil service procurement procedures and provide uneconomical social services.

The present norms for procurement pose a trade-off between red tape and corruption: red tape, while frustrating, is meant to reduce corruption. There are other ways to reach the same goal of limiting corruption without the costs of red tape, however, including stronger performance incentives for managers. Managers whose jobs and salaries depend on commercial success are less likely to accept substandard goods for a bribe.

The cost of social obligations should be made more transparent and must be accounted for explicitly in public companies' statements of performance. This will enable shareholders and the public in general to better evaluate public companies' contributions on both fronts. The subsidies to public enterprises for social services should be thought of as 'viability gap funding', to be extended to public or private infrastructure providers (or used for other pressing needs.)

A more transparent and credible subsidy regime could also encourage private companies to bid to meet social obligations.

Third, India needs to create a firewall between infrastructure incumbents and regulators. Ministers and secretaries should not serve as intermediaries between public sector companies and regulators. India's need for regulatory independence has been noted before; reducing the deterrent effect of public incumbents is one more reason to move forward.

Taming the tuskers may also require more disinvestment. Increasing the proportion of non-government shareholders creates an arms-length relationship between public companies and government backing, assuring other competitors of a fairer playing field in addition to increasing incentives for performance.

Disinvestment through a programme designed to encourage small shareholders, as has been done in countries ranging from Great Britain to Peru, will return public sector companies to the actual public.

Sacred cows move slowly. But every small step in the right direction means that the momentum forward can be that much greater. Any reform matrix must not overlook the obvious.

With Jessica Wallack
3 December 2006

24

Our Infrastructure Initiatives and the Malaise of Competitive Populism

As a run-up to the Eleventh Plan there are multiple accounts that India's drive to upgrade its infrastructure is at last 'gathering momentum'. Good news, but why are we still merely looking forward to the infrastructure boom? Why are we still merely hoping and anticipating private participation in infrastructure?

More importantly, how can we turn anticipation, a visualization of a future event, into actualization? Mental images of infrastructure get old after a while, as do the general recitations of bottlenecks and solutions. What are systematic ways to address some endemic obstacles?

We focus here on three priority concerns that are most commonly cited: payment, regulation and red tape.

First, infrastructure and service providers, particularly in the power sector, often don't get paid. Governments promise subsidy payments, but these are not fully provided for in the actual budget. Competitive populism has made user charges nearly impossible. Interstate competition is frequently cited as one of federalism's benefits—states compete to provide better policy environments to attract citizens and investors—but it cuts the other way in the states' reluctance to rationalize pricing for services such as electricity. Reductions in power tariffs for agriculture are always popular and any efforts to increase these tariffs are protested, citing examples of other states with more lenient policies.

In the long run, the best solution is market-based: public credit ratings based on past payment records and creating an incentive for good behaviour. The states' record on payment of subsidy bills to SEBs, for example, should be included in their credit ratings.

A shorter-run solution would be to guarantee subsidy payments by segregating a particular revenue source from the general budget and placing it in escrow. This has the cost of constraining expenditure management over time, but may be worthwhile.

Competitive populism poses a more significant challenge: this is part of politics in any democracy. One solution would be to limit the frequency of incentives for populism by unifying the electoral cycle. As it is, elections happen in some state every year. The inevitable pre-election promises become rallying cries for citizens in other states, bringing the whole polity into a pre-election populist mentality.

Another solution would be to enable politicians to cater to a different kind of popular demand; better infrastructure. Survey evidence, generator purchases and the survival of private water services all demonstrate consumers' willingness to pay for infrastructure and services. The underlying problem is that few governments are in a financial position to improve services before fees are collected, or in a political position to collect fees before services are improved.

Why not invest in developing an off-the-shelf model for transition loans that allow governments to improve the services up front and repay later? Indeed this was the initial rationale for the accelerated power development programme (PDP) apart from distribution improvements. Creating transparent legislation and a transition model will be useful. This should be done in conjunction with banks that are already successfully lending for local infrastructure upgrades.

Finally, another possibility for the electricity sector, where user charges are an especially significant problem, would be to guarantee extra power from central generating stations to states that rationalize pricing. The extra power allocation would enable the states to provide more reliable power in exchange for higher fees.

Second, India's regulatory environment suffers from the well-known problems of lack of independence, poor expertise and ambiguous dispute resolution.

Some parts of creating independence are simple (though not

politically easy): increase the independent budget to support a professional staff and define and respect jurisdictions.

Others are more complex. How should accountability to the public, for example, be balanced with regulatory independence? India has so far allowed regulators wide latitude in decisions, but also ensures that that decision can be reviewed by the legislature or by a special judicial review.

The rules of the game need to be made more explicit in order to attract private investment. India can also create accountability by encouraging regulators to be more transparent and explicit about their procedures and by shaping public oversight to hold commissions to these rules. Commissions should publish their conduct-of-business regulations. Judicial supervision via the TDSAT or the Electricity Appellate Tribunal should focus on the extent to which the regulators follow these procedures and not constantly subject the regulator to trials.

Finding expertise is a harder question, as there may be a trade-off between experience and impartiality. India has more than enough skilled professionals with expertise in infrastructure policy, but many of these work for the regulated industries. Higher emoluments may encourage them to serve as regulators, but would not alleviate concerns about bias. However, the talent search would necessitate closer alignment of their compensation package to prevalent market conditions.

Third, the sheer number of ministries and levels of government interested in preserving their jurisdiction over any given project leads to red tape.

The current practice of central government-created SPVs that bundle all clearances together is a stop-gap but a worthwhile beginning.

India must create stronger and more direct incentives for states to create effective one-stop shops. The central government could encourage this by providing preferential access to inputs and fuels in short supply or preferred access to financial incentives for states that either enact one-stop window or respond to applications within certain time frame. 'Naming and shaming', in which a public information centre is set up for firms to report their experiences with the governments' 'customer service' could also motivate and untangle bureaucratic tangles.

Anticipation is only exciting for so long. The malaise of competitive populism must be overcome. Well-designed policies can help the transition from competitive populism to competitive federalism.

With Jessica Wallack
19 November 2006

25

Telecom Tales: The Choice before India

How will the tale of India's telecom revolution end? India was a latecomer to mobile phones, but it is now the world's fastest-growing telecom market. Overall tele-density, including landlines and mobiles, stands at over thirteen phones per 100 persons as compared to three per 100 in 1999.

People in villages and those with low incomes too have benefited. Prepaid subscriptions, generally targeted at lower-income consumers, have grown three to four times as fast as post-paid subscriptions over the past years.

Mobile call rates, now the cheapest in the world, allow vegetable sellers to take orders, fishermen to bring their catch to the market, farmers to access market information.

But a closer look at the statistics confirms this is only a start—and a somewhat wavering start at that.

The rural–urban gap in tele-density narrowed somewhat in 2001–03, but has steadily widened since then. Rural tele-density stood at just over 5 per cent of urban tele-density at the end of 2005. The rapid expansion of access to mobile phones at the turn of the century has slowed to 5–10 per cent growth rates in the last two years.

Delhi, India's most connected city, has a tele-density comparable to Philippines or Venezuela, while rural tele-density is closer to that of Chad or the Central African Republic.

India's rapid increases in teledensity also pale in international comparison. The growth rate of mobile subscriptions over 2000–04 was comparable to the low-income country average, while the growth rate of fixed lines was lower. India's tele-density is still a fraction of any other BRIC country. The percentage of population covered by mobile phone networks has increased from 40 in 2003 to 60-65 today but is still comparable to coverage found in much of sub-Saharan Africa.

India cannot afford to be distracted or complacent. It must address the physical, technical and institutional bottlenecks that will impede future improvement and expansion of service.

First, all carriers, but especially state-owned BSNL, must invest in their networks to reduce congestion at points of interchange (POIs) between the networks. The number of POIs that did not meet TRAI's service quality standards is more than six times the number of congested POIs last year, with most of the additions on the list involving connections with BSNL.

Second, spectrum policy, a persistent bottleneck for expansion of services, has to be sorted out. Not only has military usage removed a large portion of the available spectrum from commercial use, the allocation regime has not been clear. Accusations of preferential treatment for state-owned BSNL have eroded perceptions of the regulatory environment.

TRAI's September recommendations were a welcome step towards clarification and coordination of commercial and military use of spectrum. Actually creating and empowering the suggested National Frequency Management Board would help. But the Board should be given institutional independence and resources for research on changing technology and the implications for spectrum management.

Third, TRAI must be treated as an independent regulator and accorded the resources to carry out its role effectively. The policy that emerges from the spectrum negotiations must also be technology- and provider-neutral to encourage investor entry and competition in the provision of 3G services. This is not a guaranteed outcome when regulation is subject to political pressure.

Fourth, the government should actively support service expansion in rural areas. The move to use resources in the Universal Services Obligation Fund to support rural wireless expansion is a step in the right direction. Private operators are already exploring creative ways of providing lower-cost rural services, including sharing of telecom towers, but the temporary public subsidy allowed by the Indian Telegraph Amendment Ordinance, 2006, can accelerate the process.

The programme must be implemented quickly and competitively. Most importantly, market pressures need to be maintained for the subsidized operators, perhaps by requiring operators to quote the subsidy they would require and selecting the lowest bid.

Other government resources should also be used to encourage expansion of competitive high-speed data access in rural areas. For example, the extensive fibre-optic networks of the Powergrid Corporation of India Limited and Indian Railways could be extended with last-mile connections to reach rural interiors.

These aren't trivial changes. But they will write telecom history. In one scenario, India may miss the opportunity: The dramatic growth rate will wither, rural expansion will continue to slow and the third-generation data network will never really materialize.

In the other version, public support and private initiative come together to provide a near-universal communications network for the country, bridging geographical and economic divides. India becomes a case study for the benefits of leap-frogging to the technology frontier in communications.

Our actions will now determine if the telecom revolution will really mean the death of distance for India.

Postscript

While cellphone users are increasing at a dizzy four million a month, issues connected with rural tele-density, optimizing the use of spectrum and unifying multiple taxes are challenges which need to be addressed. Devising strategies which can significantly improve rural connectivity is also critical for a faster integration on the rural economy.

With Jessica Wallack
5 November 2006

26

Economic Reform Begins with the Voter

The proposed restructuring of the Accelerated Power Development and Reform Programme (APDRP) is both timely and necessary. We all know that the financial state of distribution utilities is the Achilles' heel of the electricity sector and this programme had not gone as far as we had hoped to encourage states to reduce theft or invest in limiting technical losses. States have been slow to use the funds available for investment: a number of states completed less than half of the projects sanctioned in 2002 and only a few states have responded to the cash incentives to cut losses.

The new APDRP, with tighter restrictions on funds and stronger incentives for reform, is expected to be in place this year. One of the best changes to make would be to provide technical outreach to state electricity boards so that they are capable of defining and executing projects to take advantage of grant funds. It is not clear whether it was commitment or capacity that limited the states' use of the investment or of the incentive fund, but technical outreach could rule out the capacity excuse. This seems like a sensible strategy to deal with a complex issue that has much larger economic consequences and could be a model for other sectors, since such changes need both central- and state-level policy changes.

But we could do better. The 'carrot and stick' approach, used by the APDRP (and countless other intergovernmental incentive programmes), is one of the least subtle strategies. It assumes that states are self-contained organizations, motivated by financial incentives.

This approach contradicts the other stream of public debate about the role of states in reforms—the one that criticizes state leaders for engaging in competitive populism, lauds chief ministers as bold reformers, and presents various competitive rankings of states' policy environments. It seems to ignore one of the main arguments in favour of federalism, that sub-national governments are closer to their constituents and potentially better able to serve their area's particular preferences.

In short, incentive schemes miss an important potential motivation for reforms: the electoral preference of voters. Some governments do respond to financial incentives. All governments, in some form or other, and some more than others, respond to voter pressure.

The question, then, becomes, 'What can the centre do to activate voter pressure for states to reform?' The last phrase, 'to reform' is especially important—the subsidies saga demonstrate that electoral choice and voter pressure are not always helpful. The longer way to ask the question is: 'What can the Centre do to alter the political catalyst to channel voter pressure towards changes that may have short-term transition costs, but will ultimately improve governance, public services or economic outcomes for most of their constituents?'

Some possibilities:

- The centre can both support and demand functional transparency. In the case of APDRP, the programme should not only help states gather data from energy audits, it should encourage states to publish these data online in an easily understandable format. Subsidy support, budgeted and actual, should also be put online, along with points of reference such as costs of health clinics, teachers' salaries, etc. for comparison.
- The centre can also enable politicians to make credible 'pay for performance' bargains with citizens. At least some people are willing to pay for high-quality infrastructure: they buy generators and tanked water and so on. State officials should be enabled to provide such services reliably.
- The centre can support the independent creation of state report cards to generate competition for better governance and service quality.

- Finally, and most importantly, the centre can facilitate interstate learning of best practices, not just centre-to-state learning. NGOs and international organizations are already using such knowledge management systems.

However, the carrot-and-stick approach should not be abandoned. Sometimes voter interests at the state level are different from national interests, and sometimes state governments might need the centre to act like a heavyweight on unpopular issues. We are missing the motivation if we do not work to activate voter pressure for reform.

With Jessica Wallack
28 January 2007

27

Fear of Flying

The recent cabinet decision raising the foreign equity cap for domestic civil aviation from 40 to 49 per cent has created some excitement. This non-event was perceived to fulfil a budget promise, suggesting that civil aviation reforms were on track. It also held the prospect of some financial flows. The more meaningful recommendation of permitting equity for foreign airlines was sidestepped. Expectations have also been raised by Praful Patel's observations while receiving Part II of the Naresh Chandra Committee Report.

Civil aviation ministers characteristically have rather short tenures. While several ministers in the Atal Bihari Vajpayee government may have overstayed their welcome, we did see three civil aviation ministers. It is ironic that all three were from Bihar, which has the dubious distinction of having one of the lowest air penetrations in the country. The present incumbent is in a hurry and is not distracted by the trappings of petty patronage. India remains a difficult destination to get into and an equally difficult destination to get out of; low air-linkage density, poor infrastructure and cumbersome procedures add to its woes. Several committees have made worthwhile recommendations, not the least those contained in the Naresh Chandra Committee reports. The ills of civil aviation arise partly from our prevarication. For years, we postponed restructuring Air India and Indian Airlines or modernizing airports in the belief that they were being privatized. The civil aviation industry all over the world nosedived after 9/11. When markets were willing, we were undecided and when we decided, markets had collapsed!

The key areas which need priority attention are:

First, the short run. The benefits of airport privatization and fleet expansion will at least take two to three years to show. In the meantime, tourist traffic is rising at 30 per cent and Delhi is the venue of next year's World Travel and Tourism Council's Convention. Small investments in optimizing the use of the single runway in Delhi; operationalizing the Mumbai terminal, introducing satellite-based navigation, allocation of optimum flight levels as well as modernizing air traffic management systems will yield quick results. Improving numbers, quality and procedures for immigration management brooks no delay.

Second, to bury the hatchet of privatizing Indian Airlines and Air India, at least in the foreseeable future. They now require fleet augmentation. The leasing by Indian Airlines is primarily for replacing worn out aircraft and does not substantially augment capacities. It is amazing that proposals made by Indian Airlines three years ago for fleet acquisition first remained pending in the civil aviation ministry for eighteen months and thereafter, still awaits PIB approval. The acquisition programme for Air India is also proceeding at a tardy pace. Fear of scams makes postponement, instead of decision, a preferred option! It is appalling that proposals for enhancing the equity base of IA recommended by Kelkar years ago to compensate for the grounding of airbuses continue to languish. Given current needs, the equity of both Indian Airlines and Air India requires substantial enhancement. These can be reflected in the second supplementary to be presented to parliament in the winter session.

Civil aviation costs in India, notwithstanding the rate war between operators, are still misaligned with global costs. The single biggest factor is the fuel cost, namely aviation turbine fuel (ATF). While excise duty has been moderated, the penalty of state sales tax averaging 25 per cent is unacceptable. There will never be consensus among the states which are cash-strapped and the remedy lies in notifying ATF as 'declared goods', as was done with turbo-propelled aircraft. This has been suggested by several committees and is reflected in the Tenth Five Year Plan.

Further, airline companies should have the flexibility to import

ATF in a manner they consider the most economical. Currently, air travel in the country is cross-subsidized. The burden of servicing uneconomical routes, classified as Category II and III depending on whether they are short or long hauls, is borne by the more paying Category I routes. Route dispersal strategy should be revisited; the categorizations themselves need a second look. The broader national objective of connecting uneconomical routes should be met either directly by the budget or through a cess accruing to a non-lapsable fund, with subsidy levels being determined through competitive auctions.

The open skies policy is a bit of a misnomer. Capacity augmentation has not kept pace with traffic. The policy of bilateral rights is somewhat like 'a dog in the manger policy' because we do not have aircraft to utilize new bilateral rights and we deny these to those who may utilize them! We need to seek new arrangements.

The unutilized rights of public carriers should be auctioned to private operators while future rights acquired by the sovereign should be allocated in the most cost-effective way.

We also need to move with speed in permitting domestic private operators access to west-bound routes, even if the lucrative Middle Eastern routes are reserved for public carriers. The civil aviation industry is witnessing another demand upsurge. New orders for aircraft acquisition or leases have hardened the supply-side response. An early decision is necessary to enable private operators to effect most economical contracts.

On airports, luck must favour us. Assuming that the new lease agreements are signed by the middle of next year, visible progress will still be a few years away. The short-term issues deserve priority. Nonetheless, the joint venture process initiated must be brought to an expeditious closure.

Civil aviation improvement is at the centre of tourism, export and investment promotion. Its chequered history of broken promises fills one with weariness, if not despondency. Praful Patel is not used to flying in the air; his zest leaves some scope for an optimistic outcome. No one knows better than the prime minister and the finance minister that improved connectivity is cardinal to position India as a new economic power.

Postscript

The civil aviation reform has made heady progress. While a new civil aviation policy is still in the making and a regulator yet to be appointed, this is a sector where the UPA government has made notable progress.

First, the total number of airlines and air connectivity has increased dramatically and an open sky policy with many countries has significantly improved consumer choices and quality of connectivity. The resulting air congestion in view of inadequate infrastructure in better managing the skies has proved exasperating. Planes have to wait for long durations either to get landing permission or to secure parking bays. Hopefully these are transitional pangs that herald a better civil aviation future.

Second, Civil Aviation Minister Praful Patel's continued perseverance has resulted in Delhi and Mumbai airports being given to private contractors to upgrade existing airports and build a modern airport. Work has commenced in earnest.

A policy is also on the anvil for replicating a public–private partnership model in respect of other metro airports and smaller cities where traffic density has undergone significant increase.

Finally, the decision to merge Air India with Indian Airlines, the two public sector airlines, will improve externalities, enhance competition and benefit air travellers.

7 November 2004

28

Time to Blow the Whistle

We are often rudely jolted by a rail incident of one kind or the other: a derailment, an accident, a bridge collapse, a signal failure or a stampede. These incidents momentarily disturb us till we are distracted by some other event. The truth is, though, railway reforms are long overdue and can be postponed only at our peril. Changes will be difficult and perhaps the benefits will not be immediate, but these steps must be undertaken for enabling efficient and safe freight and passenger movement.

Some external resources, such as access to external credit of the Asian Development Bank for strengthening the Golden Quadrilateral (which, importantly, entails fulfilment of performance criteria), are in the pipeline. A special programme of Rs15,000 crore is also reportedly under the Planning Commission's consideration. Looking at the needs of Railways, however, these resources are hopelessly inadequate. The expert group on Railways estimates that the Railways will need a minimum of Rs1,30,000 crore—this is assuming a low-growth scenario that entails line augmentation, technological upgradation, network expansion, acquiring additional rolling stock, replacement including arrears and, not the least, safety requirements.

The figures for the medium and strategic high-growth rates are estimated at Rs1,60,000 and Rs2,00,000 crore respectively. The high growth rate scenario will provide the groundwork for a thorough modernization of systems in terms of speed and quality, organizational structure and its relationship with the government. The dismal financial performance of the Railways causes serious concerns and is particularly discouraging in the light of the additional resources needed.

The internal resources of the Railways which in earlier years were adequate both to meet its needs and yield dividends to the government have shrunken progressively to just 23 per cent of its requirement. Market borrowings have increased to over 30 per cent, with increased dependence on capital transfer from the general exchequer. In some years, the capital transfers have exceeded 35 per cent of their needs, and have been rising over the years. This is a recipe for financial and other disasters. Inadequacy of finance prevents adequate track upgradation, improvements in signalling systems as well as faster freight and passenger movement. It creates a vicious circle in which the inability to compete with alternative modes of transport increases, further increasing financial losses, and so on.

The pressures for Railway performance are at the same time rising. The Tenth Five Year Plan projections suggest that with 5 per cent per annum increase in freight traffic, the originating freight will increase from 489 to 624 million tonnes. A 5.7 per cent rise in passenger traffic will result in originating passengers increasing from 5000 million to 5885 million.

Successive Railway ministers, with some notable exceptions, have functioned with a populist mindset. While it is true that Railways serve a wider socio-economic purpose in providing national connectivity for men and material even in far-flung areas, the financial burden for this should be borne by transparent transfers from the General Budget so that the costs can be plainly compared to the benefits. Railways, the largest departmental undertaking, continue to function on non-commercial lines, with a distortionary tariff structure and high freight cost subsidizing passenger fare. Even non-core activities like manufacturing of wagons and coaches are being departmentally undertaken. This masks transparent accounting. Railways reform must entail the following:

- Progressive elimination of tariff distortion to enable freight movement to return to Railways, while passengers, particularly for short distances, avail of improved road connectivity. The present policy overcharges freight movement in order to subsidize ordinary passenger traffic. While freight tariffs have increased by as much as 12 per cent in a year, passenger fares have increased modestly in comparison. A tariff rebalancing carried out over a period of five years will lead to a rise of passenger revenues by about 8.6 per cent in real terms. This will require an annual adjustment of about 10 per cent increase in second-class sleeper fares and 8 per cent in second-class ordinary fares (assuming 6 per cent inflation over the next five years), saving railways some Rs4,000–5,000 crore a year and also enabling the leveraging of additional resources.

- Creating a regulatory body. Sensible tariff fixation is a political nightmare and railway ministers fear popular resentment. It would therefore be prudent to depoliticize the tariff prices through the constitution of a Railway Regulatory Authority just as has been done in the case of telecom by TRAI or in power by the CERC.
- Finishing what we have started. Railways have accumulated a large number of ongoing schemes. While programmes on track renewal, guage conversion and safety suffer financial inadequacies, new additional (favourite) projects are announced in every Railway budget. Projects which commenced in the 1970s with nominal expenditure languish in the portfolio even while new schemes are being added every year. A re-prioritization of projects within the available finances to maximize returns deserves high priority.
- Concentrating on core policies and businesses. The Railway ministry continues to combine policy functions, the provision of train services and also undertake commercial activities like running a loco factory, coach factory and canteens to name a few. Corporatization of the Indian Railways may be a distant prospect, but corporatizing these non-core activities into separate entities with transparent accounting would constitute a credible beginning. The Indian Railways must undergo major structural changes in its organization in order to confront the new competitive challenges.
- Improving speed both for freight and passenger movement in high-density corridors, particularly the Golden Quadrilateral, must receive priority. Adequacy of funds would be a challenge but

these must be fully funded both to meet freight and passenger traffic needs as well as improve finances.

The Railways remain a core infrastructure sector for sustaining our high economic growth. It requires large investments. However, resources from government or multilateral sources or market borrowing can only be available on a sustainable basis if critical pending reforms become part of this process. Laloo Prasad Yadav may have a populist profile but has the reputation to secure what he decides to achieve.

Can he reverse the decades of neglect that he inherits? A daunting challenge and opportunity awaits him. This will enhance his national profile commensurate with his political clout. It is time to blow the whistle.

Postscript

The last two Railway budgets, particularly the last one, reflect a healthy restoration of finances through vastly improved capacity utilization and reduction in the turnaround time of wagons. The dedicated freight corridors in high-density segments with public–private partnership will seek private sector managerial skills and capital in a sector which has in the past followed a turf-guarding and protectionist approach. The unprecedented economic buoyancy has no doubt helped higher volumes of passenger and freight traffic. While the current improvement and productivity gains have resulted in tariff reduction (than tariff increases) nonetheless in the long run some of the more complex issues of railway finances will need to be addressed. De-politicizing tariff fixation and creation of an independent regulatory authority remain a priority. So is the need to pursue even more aggressive public–private partnership and address other issues outlined in the Rakesh Mohan Committee report and mentioned in the approach paper of the Eleventh Plan.

5 December 2004

29

Public–Private Partnerships Are No Panacea

Public–private partnership (PPP) is in favour. Its newly discovered virtues, both at the centre and in the states endow it with almost magical qualities to resolve the multiple ills which plague our infrastructure. Therefore, the recent workshop on PPP in infrastructure industries and regulation hosted by the National Council of Applied Economic Research (NCAER) was quite timely. It brought together leading experts from reputable European institutions to interact with academics and policy makers. They covered a wide gamut of subjects like institutional capacity, forms of private partnership, the regulatory regime, financial engineering and problems in the electricity sector. The visiting experts included Paul Grout, Emmannuelle Auriol, Jerome Pouyet and Richard Portes among others. This project when completed will enhance domain knowledge on a complex set of issues where our experience is limited.

PPP is perceived to avoid the inadequacies of both the public and the private sector; the public sector is inefficient while private corporates are greedy. Excessive reliance on the former fosters inefficiency while the latter is iniquitous. In the European context, it is a mechanism for delivery of public services where the government buys services from private operators whereas in a conventional arrangement, it is the government which buys the assets and jointly builds them. In India, the press release of the finance ministry defines it as 'a project based on a contract or concession agreement, between a government or statutory entity on the one side and a private company on the other side, for delivering an infrastructure service on payment of user charges'. Similarly, the viability gap funding has been defined as 'a grant one-time or deferred, provided under this scheme with the objective of making a project commercially viable.' Typically, this mechanism supports greenfield investment and goes beyond mere hiring of private delivery services without outright privatization which implies full transfer of ownership. The virtues of this arrangement inter alia include:

- Creating fiscal space leaving adequate resources to finance other inescapable commitments on schemes which do not lend themselves to such partnership.
- Attracting private investment which may be otherwise scarce.
- Securing efficiency gains through improved private management.
- Fostering more equitable distribution of access to output and services at affordable costs.
- Creating a more competitive environment resulting in improved governance.

None of the aforesaid objectives can be pursued independent of the other nor can they be divorced from improving the overall climate for investment and sectoral reforms designed to address policy deficiencies.

The scheme for support to the PPP in infrastructure along with the features of a special purpose vehicle for funding infrastructure announced by the finance ministry in July and November 2005 broadly lays down the coverage, eligibility criteria and the approval procedures for securing the financing of infrastructure projects. Clearly, the government recognizes that 'the development of infrastructure requires large investments that cannot be undertaken out of public financing alone, and that in order to attract private capital as well as the techno-managerial efficiencies associated with it, the government is committed to promoting PPPs in infrastructure development. It is also felt that 'infrastructure projects may not always be financially viable because of long gestation periods and limited financial returns, and that the financial viability of such projects can be improved through Government support.' Within the infrastructure category, supporting the road sector would be the easiest while in other areas like power, gas pipeline and special economic zones, the pace of progress would be conditioned by the sectoral reforms.

However, excessive enthusiasm for a PPP approach must recognize the complexities of several issues:

First, intrinsically, this is a sub-optimum solution. It recognizes that public consensus for outright privatization remains elusive but partnering the private sector is socially more acceptable. However, these special arrangements are no substitute to ongoing sector reforms. There is inherent danger that redressing endemic sector-specific issues, particularly on subsidies and tariffs, get postponed under the pretext that investments are being secured by this special mechanism. For instance, implementation of mega power projects is no substitute to resolving issues of open access, enhanced competition, elimination of distortionary cross-subsidies, to name a few.

Second, evolving a model concessionaire agreement, in which risk assignment and unbundling combine the virtues of equity and efficiency, needs to be benchmarked so that they are at par with the best international practice as well as the stage of the sector-specific reforms. There could be wide variations across sectors, regions and states.

Third, ensuring the quality of service as stipulated in the concessionaire agreement is always problematic. Assuming adequacy of the monitoring mechanism, short-term contractual arrangements may not secure financial closure while longer-term contracts make ensuring service quality and penalty imposition more difficult.

Fourth, the application of user charges which combines financial viability with distributional and equity considerations makes tariff rebalancing a complex issue. The time frame for application of market-based user charges and its calibration during the transition period needs consultation and consensus of stakeholders. Market imperfections and asymmetry of information can create serious moral hazard concerns during the transition period.

Finally, regulatory and legal issues are critical. While some of this is embedded in the broader context of our legal reforms, alternative measures of dispute resolution and contract enforcement would remain a precondition for securing large private flows.

The PPP is at a nascent stage. We must get these issues right for making it a powerful tool for infrastructure improvement. Enticing private investment and improving managerial efficiency would be dependent on how credibly these concerns are addressed. However, PPP is not a panacea for our multiple infrastructure ills. There are no fixed paradigms on the most preferred modes of such arrangement. We can shape it to meet our needs and more broad-based reforms would make the transition more acceptable.

16 April 2006

VI

ENERGY

30

The Energy Paradigm: Back to the Future

A few days ago, Prime Minister Manmohan Singh spoke at the meeting of the advisory council on trade and industry on the need to depoliticize energy pricing. This reminder is none too early. Non-market-based energy pricing distorts choices consumers and firms make about how much, and what type of energy to use. These sentiments were also echoed at a BBC-sponsored discussion on the 'energy challenge' at the recent India Economic Summit of the World Economic Forum. The round table discussion in which I participated covered a gamut of subjects from energy pricing, demand–supply balances, environmental consequences to the need for greater R&D in affordable and environmentally friendly sources of energy.

Consider the following facts:

- While energy intensity—the energy consumption needed for a given amount of growth—is expected to marginally improve (decrease) by 1.2 per cent per year in industrial economies and 1.8 per cent in the developing countries, the overall magnitude of energy use will rise. (Figures are from the *International Energy Outlook* (*IEO*).
- The *IEO* projects that world-marketed energy consumption will increase by 54 per cent before 2025, with the fastest growth in consumption from India and China. Developing Asia (including India and China) will account for 40 per cent of this increase.

- India will consume over five million barrels of oil a day by 2030, over double its current consumption.
- India itself, the world's sixth-largest energy consumer, currently relies on coal for more than half of its total energy needs.

We can clearly see that fossil fuels drive the economy and that the need for this fuel will increase over the coming decades. The projected supply of oil, and importantly, the limits of supply, however, depend on the assumptions made and the methodology employed in making these calculations. M. Hubbert predicted in 1949 that 'the oil age would be short', and reiterated this basic message through his career. The *World Energy Outlook* (*WEO*) now projects that supply will be fine up to 2030, but there are uncertainties beyond. The deadlines have been progressively extended as new technologies for exploration and extraction are developed. Nevertheless, the cost of extraction will continue to rise. The June 2004 *National Geographic* argued credibly that the 'end of cheap oil' is in sight.

Coal and natural gas reserves are projected to last longer—one estimate of natural gas availability from the *WEO* notes that we have sixty-six more years' worth (at current production) of natural gas available.

Whatever the deadline for depletion, or at least the point at which the energy required to extract fossil fuels exceeds the energy content of the fuels, hydrocarbon resources are finite. The depletion of oil in particular will alter economic activity—both in terms of the cost of energy as an input as well as the availability of essential petrochemical compounds used in plastics, availability of fertilizer and other everyday materials.

The environmental consequences of continued dependence on fossil fuels are perhaps more immediate. Global emissions are likely to grow at 62 per cent over the next three years and the developing countries will overtake the developed economies by 2020. Even though emission intensity, i.e., emission per growth of unit, is expected to decline, there will be severe consequences arising out of inevitable climate changes resulting from global warming.

Regardless of what version of the doomsday scenario one accepts, or what timeline one believes, we need to now begin to develop policies to ensure future prosperity.

First, we need to diversify the likely risks due to environmental changes. Some areas will get warmer, others colder. Some areas will see rainfall increase, others will see a decrease. Even if the new climate is not unbearable, the adjustment of infrastructure usage and lifestyle to newer locations would entail significant transitional costs, both economic and human. The sea level will rise, affecting coastal areas (including low-lying cities such as Mumbai). Weather models provide some indication of the impact of warming, but there is still great uncertainty. The challenge is to develop appropriate insurance schemes and contracts.

Second, we need to stem the impact that energy use has on the environment. We must provide a mechanism to internalize the positive externalities of sustainable energy use. Currently, the costs of more efficient or environmentally sound technologies are borne by individuals, while environmental benefits are spread round the world. There is little incentive to switch to new technologies or conserve energy. How does one get consumers and industries to internalize the costs of energy use? One critical factor would be to encourage a move to efficiency based on the domestic pricing of electricity. It is essential to have prices that reflect the cost of energy while encouraging consumers to make the right decision as well as international arrangements on how to cap emissions and at the same time permit firms to trade emission rights.

Third, there will be huge investments needed for extracting raw energy resources and building related infrastructure with rising costs. The *IEO* projects an investment requirement of USD 500 billion. Financing this huge investment will be a major challenge and resources will only be forthcoming if pricing distortions are minimized.

Fourth, we need to strengthen diplomatic alliances and agreements to provide a framework for allocation and supply chains for increasingly scarce resources. The *WEO* estimates that 85 per cent of the increase in production of primary energy over the next two decades will take place outside of the OECD. Gas reserves are heavily concentrated in Russia, the Middle East and the countries in transition. Energy users are generally located elsewhere, creating challenges for linking these two groups across political jurisdictions.

Fifth, it is time to appreciate the limitations of continuing dependence on conventional energy sources and move towards new technology to fill this gap. Governments can foment R&D in the short run with an enabling fiscal package, but only a sensible pricing policy can incentivize research and innovation.

We would need to effectively address the multiplicity of economic and environmental challenges. The changing energy paradigm compels us to get 'back to the future'.

Postscript

Issues of energy security and climate change dominate the global debate. The report of the expert committee under Nicholas Stern submitted to the government of the United Kingdom highlights climate change vulnerabilities and suggests that a tipping point could be reached soon if we do not get our act together quickly and spend a modest 1 per cent of global GDP. Scientific evidence that climate change is man-made rather than a reflection of long-term cycles is more generally accepted. There are controversies on discount rates used by Stern in calculating the financial outcomes. The subsequent report of the inter-governmental report on climate change under the chairmanship of R.K. Pachauri submitted in Paris three weeks ago has further reiterated global concerns on the consequences of climate change. The centrepiece of the recent Davos Summit 2007 was also climate change. International opinion is veering around on the need to hasten action, put in additional resources and seek lifestyle changes. The fact that the Kyoto Protocol will expire in 2012 and will need to be renewed by a substitute agreement and modalities to bring within its fold the United States and Australia remains worrisome. The extent to which developing countries like India and China, who are and will increasingly become important users of fossil fuel, can remain exempted from undertaking quantitative obligations has reopened some settled issues.

A pollution tax remains controversial.

One hopes that a slight moderation in oil price will not lull us into complacency in the face of mounting evidence on the devastating impact of changes in habitation and activity patterns. These along with other changes will inflict untold human misery. It is therefore necessary to begin tangible action within a time-bound programme without further delay.

12 December 2004

31

Energy Prices Vs Global Warming

Global warming is in sharp focus. The Kyoto Protocol, namely, the UN Framework Convention on Climate Change, enacted in 1997, comes to an end in 2012. The international community of 190 governments is currently meeting in Germany for its extension; though agreement on multiple emission-control targets is not in sight. The United States, the world's biggest polluter, did not join this international treaty. It has other ideas about reversing global warming.

In the meantime, excessive emission of carbon dioxide continues to affect millions—changing weather patterns, increasing incidence of floods with arid zones becoming drier, wet regions becoming wetter, and threatened submergence through rising sea levels.

Scientific evidence attributes global warming to the excessive use of fossil fuel and related carbon dioxide emissions. And yet we are anxious that high fuel prices might stall the sunshine of continued economic buoyancy. There is hesitation everywhere to pass on the high prices of petro-products to end-use consumers. President Bush in his State of the Union address in January, while describing Americans as excessive guzzlers of fossil fuels, does not want gasoline prices to be raised which could moderate consumption. In fact, taxes are being calibrated lest high gasoline prices hurt the outcome of the November elections. Dick Cheney, speaking in Vitrius, accused Russia of practising energy blackmail by extracting high prices. That the Russians are consolidating their influence in the Central European countries and are not averse to leveraging their energy power is no secret.

Nonetheless, the Russian plea that higher prices are the outcome of progressively applying market-based principles has fallen on deaf ears. At the recently concluded spring meeting of the IMF and the World Bank, as well as the annual general meeting of the Asian Development Bank, there was unanimity that the main exogenous risk to sustained global growth was the unforeseen consequences of high energy prices.

Thus, while India is not alone in attempting to protect consumers, its excessive politicization is quite unique. Everyone is aware that we went through a period when prices were becoming increasingly market-determined till Ram Naik in the earlier government discovered that there was a need for consensus among NDA partners. The present government had no difficulty in fully accepting this and making it even more onerous because consultations now mean consensus not only within the cabinet (and the warring ministries) but with all allied partners.

What is now being proposed is hopelessly inadequate to fill the large hole of over Rs 73,000 crore created in the finances of oil companies. How long can the budget absorb this? Of course, the high prices of crude have conferred windfall revenue gains and part of this could be shared to mitigate the burden on the consumers. However, the general practice of calibrating duty rates to compensate for price volatility is scarcely rational. In good times, oil companies can create a price stabilization fund and protect its corpus from being integrated with the budget. The proposal on oil bonds may ease liquidity pressures but constitute borrowing and contingent liability, which must be reckoned in fiscal numbers.

Going beyond the current debate, the issue is more basic, namely, how to sustain economic growth in an era of high energy prices? Some of the answers are obvious. First and foremost, to increasingly price products at the economic cost and confine subsidies through cleverer financial engineering to the really needy and those below the poverty line. Second, to re-engineer products and processes which are low on energy intensity. A conscious policy which discourages high energy-intensive activity will incentivize labour-intensive technologies. No doubt, the absence of flexible labour policies inhibits the adoption of technologies best suited to our factor endowments.

Third, energy efficiency needs vastly improved commitment and implementation. Currently, it is administered by the power ministry which has no serious stake in the pricing of petroleum products except gas for power. The implementation of the Energy Efficiency Act needs closer monitoring.

Fourth, far greater emphasis on R&D in alternative fuels—dual fuel policies must become more attractive. A start-up in Tennessee is marketing stills that can be set up as private distilleries making ethanol out of fermented starchy crops such as corn, apples or sugarcane, and claims that the pump price of gasoline can be cut by a third. This is a direction in which we need to move more aggressively.

Fifth, we need to have a floor price on a barrel of oil which could be part of our comprehensive energy security policy. Only this can incentivize long-term investment in yields, flex fuel vehicles and distribution outlets for alternative fuels.

In the end, it would be hypocritical to talk of high global warming and high oil prices in the same breath. Global warming is primarily a result of excessive fossil fuel use which is induced by low energy prices. If people pay market-related prices for energy, they will learn to readapt activities and lifestyles to conserve energy and also to arrest the escalation of global warming. As long as we continue to believe that fossil fuel energy is either abundant or more sophisticated technologies make their extraction viable and overlook demand moderation as concomitant to supply elasticities, concerns on global warming will remain peripheral. The malignant side of this asymmetry is that we may neither have cheap oil nor contain climate change. Efficient energy pricing is the inescapable principle on which rests the future of sustainable economic growth. Combining prosperity with acceptable environmental management is never easy.

21 May 2006

32

Oil's Well That Doesn't End Well

We must recognize that energy must be priced at its economic cost and subsidies either by oil companies (which are anyway owned by the government) or the government themselves be transparently funded. For decades, the government had been in the business of micro-managing petroleum prices but formally got out of it by dismantling the administered price regime (APM) in 1997. Diesel was moved to import parity price with an approved phased programme of dismantling the subsidy on kerosene and LPG, and during the transition the budget directly bore the subsidy burden. The NDA regrettably brought back the APM instead of leaving these decisions to oil companies. Ram Naik delighted himself in TV appearances informing us of the emerging consensus within the NDA on prospective price increases. The UPA government has perpetuated this distortion. Mani Shakar Aiyar is one of the brightest ministers of this government with a sound understanding of economics. Television appearances justifying every paise increase in petroleum prices or for postponing decisions mask the truth that these exogenous events are beyond government control and that subsidies, more often than not, do not reach the intended beneficiaries. Illustratively, the kerosene subsidy has generated a new commercial enterprise for profitable adulteration rather than lighting poor homes. Subsidy targeting for the poor is a key challenge. The plain fact is that prices today are calibrated at around US$ 28–30 a barrel whereas oil companies are contracting supplies at US$ 38–40 a barrel. The difference of US$10–

12 a barrel must be paid by users or substantially by users with the balance coming out of budget support. The failure to do so is severely impacting the financial health of oil companies. Indian Oil registered a 31per cent fall in its second-quarter profits. The full-year earnings of Indian Oil may drop by 4 per cent while Hindustan Petroleum and Bharat Petroleum may also register a 3 per cent decline. Oil companies are in financial distress.

The option of mitigating the burden on the consumer through duty adjustments cannot be pursued perennially and aimlessly. Aimless because duty structures must reflect long-term fiscal policy directions and not ad hoc responses to unexpected price volatility. Perennial because budget-making is an annual exercise and barring important events, major duty changes should be part of the budget-making process. The Lahiri Committee's recommendations expected by end-November should not be pre-empted by major duty adjustments merely to avoid taking the more sensible decision on price increases.

Fiscal policies should be predictable and stable to attract large investments for the development of hydrocarbons.

Our approach should reflect four key considerations.

First, on the demand side. We should lower the demand curve by allowing price elasticities to operate through appropriate pricing of the products. In passing the burden substantially to the consumer, we can always differentiate segments which we wish to protect through continuation of subsidies and these should be borne by the budget.

Second, the UPA government is rightly committed to strengthening the health of PSUs through managerial and financial autonomy. It would be ironic if the government, while guaranteeing autonomy, continues to micro-manage key price decisions which are central to their working.

Third, the Energy Efficiency Bill and the Energy Audit functions need not remain ceremonial instruments. An implementation plan should be drawn and implemented with vigour. Energy conservation should be a national priority in the light of the current oil scenario.

Fourth, on the supply side, fullest encouragement is necessary for the implementation of the New Exploration Licensing Policy

(NELP). A regulator for both the upstream and downstream of the hydrocarbon sector is a matter of priority; the ministry should not become the micro-managers of commercial exploration decisions. Mani's aggressive oil diplomacy needs our fullest support for enabling both the public and private sectors to acquire oil equities abroad and explore options on new sources of energy. We also need not be inhibited by our deep-seated reservations on the security of transit routes to harness the large reserves of Iran and other Central Asian Republics.

Finally, we need an integrated energy policy which moves away from excessive dependence on fossil fuel-based energy. Kirit Parikh is working on the contours of this new energy policy. Montek Singh Ahluwalia himself, and subsequently I, had overseen the steering group on integrated energy policy in the context of the Tenth Plan. We also need to harmonize the sometimes asymmetric interest of various ministries of coal, petroleum, power, non-conventional energy and nuclear power. The economic options of non-conventional energy sources need fresh consideration in the light of current price trends. Low-energy-intensive activity, particularly in services, where we have a comparative factor advantage deserves particular encouragement. I would urge the creation of a cabinet committee on energy under the prime minister which can oversee the implementation of an integrated energy plan.

High energy costs will stay with us and ad hoc responses detract sensible decision making. Mani is too clever not to realize that petroleum pricing cannot be pursued through the Panchayati Raj model of excessive consultations. The world, as well as India, must adjust to an era of high energy cost.

Postscript

An administrative price regime is back in fashion. Depoliticizing the price of petroleum products is on the back-burner. Ad hoc measures like the issue of oil bonds, tinkering with customs and excise duties are being undertaken to protect the consumer from the volatility of price behaviour. These fail to address long-term concerns. Phasing out subsidies and moving to the market-related price of fossil fuels, particularly in the context of climate change, remain unaddressed.

31 October 2004

33

The Elusive Goal of Energy Security

Energy issues are in sharp focus. The 'State of the Union' address by President Bush, preceded by former president, Bill Clinton's remarks in Davos are being interpreted as America's growing unease with both the economics and politics of energy management. The recent visit of the US undersecretary for energy resulted in better delineation of the Indo-US energy partnership. The Observer Research Foundation (ORF) in a conclave on 'Major Challenges for India's Energy Security' brought together Indian and foreign experts as well as policy-makers for wide-ranging interactions. Montek Singh Ahluwalia, who inaugurated the conclave, appropriately observed that discussions on energy security can only be meaningful in the context of energy policies and succinctly commented on our key concerns. The centrality of the pricing issue and of balancing the need to let markets decide while protecting the consumers from excessive volatility remain a difficult challenge. The modalities of such protection through income transfers, or keeping prices low by calibrating subsidies, or merely doing so for a target group do not offer clear acceptable options. In the presentations made by Robert Mabro, president of the Oxford Institute of Energy Studies, Paul Bradley, Paul Stevens and others seemed to converge on two issues—a prognosis that oil prices in the medium term will remain high, above US$ 58; and the need to use energy more efficiently, diversify risks through better demand and supply management and look for alternative fuels.

It is believed that the current 'supply constraints' are the result of investment adequacies and given leads and lags, policy design must factor persistent price volatility. In his interventions, Xia Yishan, director of the Energy Research Centre, China, confessed enhanced competition to foreclose global energy supplies, but did not, per se, perceive it to be unhealthy. George Andersen, former Canadian deputy minister of natural resources, suggested an international coalition of interest on energy, particularly coal. OPEC must engage in dialogue with major users, but putting aside differences may not be easy. Similarly, despite large coal resources, the contours of global cooperation and sharing of technologies need an energetic group to act as a trigger. The interaction encouraged R.K. Mishra, chairman, ORF to announce an annual energy conference, as well as an India energy report; improved database will make discussions more informed.

One of the immediate provocations for the ORF conference was the Kirit Parikh report on 'Integrated Energy Policy'. The report touches on many complex issues, but understandably, doesn't have answers to many of them. A credible policy to determine inter se fuel pricing policy, regulator harmonization, depoliticizing tariff and also reflect the costs of huge R&D investment elsewhere in non-conventional energy—both by public and private institutions—is necessary but difficult. Besides, ownership for implementing its daunting recommendations needs clearer delineation. Thus, improving power availability will remain our principal challenge even while we improve energy efficiency, seek alternatives, diversify supply sources and intensify domestic exploration.

The prime minister has more than once recognized the importance of power reforms. The proposed meeting of chief ministers would be more purposive after the elections in several states. Of course, this provides only a window of opportunity before the state elections next year. Since 73 per cent of power comes from coal, the reform of this sector is critical. The woes of coalition politics stymied the recent opportunity to induct a younger, talented minister for this sector. Action must include amendment of the Coal Mines Nationalization Act to facilitate private participation, the removal of coal from the essential commodities list, enhancing private participation, spinning off profitable coal companies as independent corporate entities, and an independent regulatory authority for allocation, exploitation and price determination. Pursuing the daunting agenda on power reforms needs both tact and patience. While the central regulator has made a credible beginning, faster adoption of open access, minimizing the wide variations on cross-subsidy surcharge, rationalizing trading margins, instituting multi-year tariffs are some areas where further action is necessary. Power reforms by way of operationalizing the Electricity Act, 2003, the announcement of a Tariff and Electricity Policy, renewed emphasis on privatization of distribution, improved audit of transmission and distribution losses and fostering large investment proposals constitute worthwhile progress—given federal complexities. Nonetheless, the financial performance of the state power sector remains a major concern, where the rate of return at -28.1 per cent in 2005–06 is only marginally lower than what it was five years ago at -32.8 per cent; or losses of Rs 22,013 crore last year somewhat higher than what it was in 2002–03!

There is no alternative to pursuing distribution reforms with renewed vigour aimed at faster deregulation, even while protecting the genuine poor through a combination of measures. We know this is a long haul and there are no magic answers. Power reforms must proceed in tandem with the reform of coal, oil and gas—both on pricing and regulatory issues. However, neither these nor perceived market imperfections can become a ruse for tardy power reforms. Increasing volumes of power which are tardy or seeking faster private distribution remain merely convenient policy slogans. Tokenism is no substitute to a credible roadmap.

In the end, energy security implies mitigation of risks. While this encompasses efficient demand management, diversifying both sources and forms of energy, it must be underpinned with credible sector reforms. For too long, these reforms have been caught in the quagmire of debilitating electoral politics. This more than anything else makes energy security an elusive goal.

18 February 2006

34

We Need to Manage Supply Better

Oil prices have softened with analysts projecting further downward adjustment. If this is true, a significant risk for sustained global growth is mitigated. Nonetheless, the long-term inequilibrium between demand and supply of fossil fuel, coupled with environmental risks, will continue to exert upward pressure on oil prices. Contributing to this in no small measure will be the increase in demand from emerging markets like India and China.

Hopefully, the fall in oil prices will not lull us into complacency and make us neglect key energy concerns. Quite a few of these are mentioned in the Kirit Parikh report on integrated energy policy. In this essay, I will focus on supply management and regulatory oversight. The supply side recommendations in the report are a mixed basket: it is indeed a difficult and complex task to deregulate and regulate primary energy sources, given the long history of public dominance and a variety of interests involved, but it is also essential to get it right. Notwithstanding the current hype on alternative energy forms, the report is candid enough to admit that 'even if India succeeds in exploiting its full hydro potential of 1,50,000 MW, the contribution of hydro energy to the energy mix will only be around 1.9–2.2 per cent'. It is clarified that the hydro share in the primary energy mix comes out lower because of the way oil equivalence of hydroelectricity is calculated.

Similarly 'if a twenty-fold increase takes place in India's nuclear power capacity by 2031–32, the contribution of nuclear energy to

India's energy mix is at best expected to be 4–6.4 per cent'. In short, the management of coal remains critical in the short and even in the medium term. From this point of view one is tempted to ask, why is there so little deregulation in the coal sector? The proposal is to allow coal blocks that CIL can't bring into production by 2016–17 to go to 'other eligible candidates' for development by 2011–12. But given the general tendency to set targets higher than achievements, at what point will CIL admit that it will not bring these blocks online by 2016? Will this be early enough for the 'other eligible candidates' to bring them online? How realistic are the proposals to allow private entry? Coal exploration is still being done only by the Central Mine Planning and Design Institute, which has meant that estimates have been slower to come and are somewhat unreliable. The Coal Mines Denationalization Bill, 2000, has been pending in parliament for six years. In the meantime, the government has merely been allowing private companies to exploit the coal for power generation. Besides, it is hardly encouraging that language about private participation seems to have been diluted from the draft NIEP, which had proposed that 'finally, isolated deposits of all hydrocarbons including coal may be tapped economically through sub leases to the private sector'.

Draft National Integrated Energy Policy (NIEP), Railways, and their role in transporting coal from pit head to power plant, are not mentioned in the coal section. Why not? Nor is the option of improving power transmission lines to bring power from pit head plants elsewhere been considered, if the coal itself cannot be moved. Similarly for gas, it can be simply put: the best way to encourage exploration to expand local supply is to allow private companies to charge market prices for the gas they discover. The current approach on regulated prices with a 'fair' return until some of the potential reserves become available is unlikely to be effective. Volatility remains an important issue. Some degree of shelter from volatility is important. However, simply setting prices as the average of several months is not necessarily the best way to do it. This essentially makes the government bear the risk as it smoothes the price.

Why not allow users of primary energy to engage in forward contracts to hedge their prices? Or to expand the types of contracts they offer to their consumers who may have varying degrees of tolerance for risk? This will creates a private market for risk and risk reduction. On fuel pricing, the idea that 'in a competitive set up, the marginal use value of different fuels, which are substitutes, should be equal at a given place and time so that the price of different fuels at different places do not differ by more than the cost of transporting the fuels,' may not be the best guide for policy. This is a long-run statement about the choice of fuels. Fuels may be substituted over the long run, but in the short run (which could be on a scale of years), specific choices about conversion of fuel to electricity or transport or other uses have been made so that fuels are not direct substitutes. The marginal use values are unlikely to be the same at any point in time. What is more important is to provide some means of clarity and transparency that enables the market to reasonably project long-run shifts in fuel prices and make decisions about investments based on these. The more political and regulatory uncertainty there is, the more these resource allocation decisions will remain skewed.

There are three other issues, which at the very least, deserve a brief comment.

- The Committee has suggested the creation of a national energy fund (NEF) to finance R&D on the alternative forms of energy excluding atomic energy, which is being separately funded. This is proposed by a special levy. I am somewhat hesitant to accept that we add one more cess to an already long list.
- The report has proposed a subsidy by entitling directed households to thirty units a month of kerosene and LPG purchases up to six kg through a system of debit card. In principle, rationalizing subsidies through better targeting of the intended beneficiaries is sensible. The implementation mechanism needs to be carefully worked out in consultation with state governments.
- Finally, it is a pity that the terms of reference of the committee left out the issue of regulatory oversight. Conflicting regulatory regimes and the absence of a super-regulator for energy will be a serious handicap in implementing an integrated energy policy. On the whole, the new focus on energy, particularly on the need for an integrated approach is welcome. But what is the path forward and the assurance that a softer oil regime and other

distractions will not push this to a back-burner? Energy security does remain critical in our quest for sustained development.

Postscript

The Kirit Parikh report has since been received. While it contains many sensible recommendations, the ownership on its implementation remains unclear. Fragmented responsibilities over a number of departments and ministries will not result in purposive coherent action.

1 October 2006

VII

REFORMS

35

The Illusion of Public Sector Autonomy Making a Beginning

Disinvestment, much less privatization, is clearly out of fashion. Chidambaram, irrespective of what he privately believes, has ruled out strategic sales. In fact, he reiterated what was decided in February 2005. Incremental disinvestment may yield much needed resources either for a dedicated corpus or to support social outlays but inhibits multiplier productivity gains of deeper action. Disinvestment has been on a roller coaster ride; commencing by bundling of shares to nominal disinvestment to aggressive (sometimes mindless) privatization now followed by incremental dilution.

The approach represents the prevalent ideological predilections, not necessarily the dictates of economic logic. Whenever disinvestment is on the back-burner, the autonomy of public enterprises becomes the frontrunner. However, PSU autonomy is intrinsically important for sustaining growth momentum irrespective of privatization. The previous government in its zest for privatization ignored strengthening PSUs, and while only some companies were contemplated for privatization, there was persistent uncertainty with respect to others. Privatization is not an all-embracing panacea nor can all public undertakings, both central and states, be privatized in the foreseeable future. Public undertakings are in a broad category, ranging from commercial operations to the provision of social goods; their improvement creates gainful virtuous circles.

So how do they improve?

The cabinet, in July 2005, took some important decisions to increase the flexibility and autonomy of public undertakings by raising the cap on financial exposure for Navratna or Mini-Ratna companies, either for greenfield investments or in joint ventures. The decision followed the recommendations of the Adhoc Group of Experts on Empowerment of Public Sector Enterprises, headed by Dr Arjun Sengupta.

By the mid-1990s, with increased liberalization, it was generally recognized that public enterprises could not compete effectively with private entrepreneurs without freedom to function and operate commercially. The lowering of tariffs and the dismantling of quantitative restrictions enhanced competitiveness vis-à-vis efficient large global players. Thus, in July and October 1997, the concept of Navratna and Mini-Ratna was introduced with greater delegated authority, both financial and managerial. The Arjun Sengupta report, in line with the National Common Minimum Programme, makes wide-ranging recommendations. However, what are the key concerns?

First, the notion of autonomy to public undertakings is linked with improved governance. Genuine autonomy could make many ministers jobless. Several ministries are almost exclusively engaged in dabbling in what should be left to the corporates; sometimes inventing, if not reinventing, work under the garb of improved supervision. Think of a coal minister who cannot favour a preferred industrialist with raw material linkage or help a contractor of Coal India so as to return past favours, or a civil aviation minister unable to nudge a bilateral air agreement and remain oblivious of a large fleet acquisition, or a petroleum minister unconcerned about the selection of a joint venture partner by oil companies.

Sometimes the distinction between what constitutes a policy issue that makes ministerial engagement legitimate and that which remains dominantly in the commercial domain is opaque.

Discretion about what would be appropriate will remain a judgmental issue and depend on the good sense of the dramatis personae at the helm of affairs.

The truth is that for several decades, public undertakings have been increasingly used by successive ministers to exercise power and patronage which the ministries themselves neither have nor can confer. The CVC rightly put a brake in some instances. Coalition politics limits flexibility to reform the government and yet PSU reforms are embedded in governance reform. The inculcation of a mindset necessitated by competitive market economics is not easy.

Second, some important suggestions by the Sengupta Committee on what the government must abstain from doing (a kind of negative list) includes pricing and distribution, export and import, the award of contracts and the selection of joint venture partners. These are far-reaching. Their implementation is not in sight. Needless to say, autonomy is meaningless without enabling corporates to take tariff and pricing decisions in their best commercial judgement. Any subsidy for broader welfare considerations must be borne by the budget, not by the company.

The present controversy on price increase in petroleum products is a telling example of what must not happen. Cross-subsidies on petroleum, railway tariff, coal and issue price of foodgrains are distortionary and strike at the root of commercial autonomy. On award of contracts, transparency of the process, the best international practice, a study of the evolving market trends and objective data analysis are critical in resisting political interference.

Third, the decision-making processes of public undertakings—notwithstanding change in respect of Navratna and Mini-Ratna—remain complex. The role of the finance ministry (public investment board), the planning commission and the cabinet committee on economic affairs (CCEA) needs to be redefined to impart genuine autonomy and suit the needs of our times.

Fourth, on the appointment of the chairman and the board of directors, a radical change is needed. Since the government remains the principal shareholder, it must appoint the chairman. However, the appointment of directors can be left to the board of directors. Further, the practice of non-official directors being shuffled around and chosen from men of indifferent quality, depending on the political preference of the government in office, must be discontinued. Non-official directors must add value to the company. Guidelines should be issued by the government but the search and selection must be left to the board. There is one more aspect in selecting a suitable chairman or director. If Navratnas and Mini-Ratnas are to compete with the best from the private sector, they must choose quality talent; looking for insiders or those with prior government experience may not be adequate. Government salary structures and the conditions of work inhibit choice since the search net cannot be cast wide enough, nor can it attract the best talent. Within the framework of the government retaining the 51 per cent share, the issue of securing the best talent for public companies needs an innovative solution.

Fifth, excessive administrative control through elaborate layers of supervision, within the framework of parliamentary accountability, must be eased. The expert group has made numerous suggestions on redefining parliamentary accountability but their implementation will remain daunting.

Finally, there is one suggestion made by the committee which is clearly bad. The suggestion to create six overarching supervisory boards will only add a new administrative layer and kindle fresh passion for bureaucratic and political interference. It will result in disempowerment instead of empowerment.

A credible beginning has been made on imparting autonomy to public undertakings. The government must divest itself of obligations to determine prices, fix tariffs, meddle in contracts and micro-manage appointments. The advocacy by the chairman of the expert group with coalition partners and his friends among the allies will enable consensus building. His recent election to the House of Elders multiplies the onerousness of his obligations. Autonomy so far has remained an illusion. Only these tangible actions can make it a reality.

21 August 2005

36

Patents Act: Not a Magic Bullet but a Necessary Pill

The recent ordinance promulgated by the government amends the Patents Act to provide for product patents covering pharmaceuticals, chemicals and food. This is in compliance with the Trade Related Aspects of Intellectual Property Rights (TRIPS) obligation undertaken in the WTO. India has an enviable record of fully adhering to its international obligations. It has done so even in the midst of a balance of payment crisis; India has never turned away from its debt, sought a rescheduling or a waiver. Adhering to the date of 1 January 2005 is part of this consistency. Nothing is lost because on the one hand we have adhered to our commitment and on the other, the parliament will fully debate the bill in the house or its standing committee.

The patents ordinance has not pleased anyone. It may well be that since all parties are equally unhappy, the statute appropriately balances the rights and obligations of all stakeholders! Consumers fear that it may lead to price hikes making medicines unaffordable for the poor. However, a clarification that only an insignificant percentage of medicines is likely to be covered, that the law is prospective and that the Drug Price Control Order will continue should help allay misgivings.

The domestic industry fears that increased competition, import surges, the deep pockets of the MNCs constitute a non-level playing field. However, the pharma industry in India has come of age, has enjoyed the benefits of 'reverse engineering' for long, is seeking global opportunities and is well poised to face enhanced competition. Large pharma companies, including foreign ones, fear that the new Act does not provide adequate protection, the loopholes are large, its application is only prospective, patent procedures remain cumbersome and compulsory licensing provisions are unduly open-ended and its application to new innovations overly restrictive.

Some of these concerns deserve fuller consideration and hopefully the ensuing debate in parliament will iron out these wrinkles. The pharmaceutical industry in India has made rapid strides, sheltered partly by the absence of a product patent regime which has permitted specialization in reverse engineering—often a polite word for 'successful copying'. Be that as it may, it has served an important social purpose in making medicines available at costs which are significantly lower than even Pakistan's. Indian companies are well positioned to expand their global presence based on growing competitiveness, a strong manufacturing base, and the availability of skilled manpower and an expanding biotech industry. Low investments in research and development (R&D), the absence of dynamic linkages between industry and academia, absence of a culture that encourages innovation and inadequate regulatory standards will be handicaps.

It is, however, worthwhile to examine the basic design of the proposed patent regime.

Why are patents necessary? The economic rationale behind patents lies in giving pioneer firms lead time to recoup costs invested in R&D. This assumes that innovative firms have significant sunk costs which cannot be recovered by mere realization of marginal costs, which are low. The problem with drugs is that they are a high-fixed-cost industry with low marginal costs. The high fixed costs are also uncertain and dependent on the effort and expertise of scientists, which makes them difficult to determine. The fixed cost of any successful drug might not be so high, but this is not what the investor sees ex-ante. Other than the fixed cost of a successful drug, he must also reckon with the probability of success among many failures. So what does this mean? Competition would ordinarily drive the cost of the drug down to the marginal cost so that the fixed cost could not be apportioned and recovered. So there may be no investment. This is why we have patents in the first place. But then the question is: Do patents apportion the 'fixed costs' equitably? And do they ensure that the drug companies retain zero economic profits as they would in competition (in other words, collect fixed plus marginal costs only, nothing more)? Not necessarily.

As far as apportioning fixed costs goes, does equitably mean evenly? So that everyone pays the same price? Or does equitable mean according to means? Which implies some kind of restricted distribution that would be difficult to protect from opportunism. This is a difficult question, related to subsidy design. But keeping prices to a minimum while allowing fixed cost recovery is a matter of patent design. And here the difficulty is that actual fixed costs are not observable and can be manipulated. So if you offered a kind of cost-plus regime, in which the patent for an individual drug allowed the company to recover its stated costs, no more, no less, then you would have the typical cost-plus problem. But then if you offer a flat fee, or a flat protected period, then you are either over-rewarding the producer (having easy performance measures in performance-based pricing) or stifling investment. How to balance and walk the line between these two sides without knowing what the costs really are, or the lowest they could be if the patent got the incentives right? It's not as if the drug companies will ever say 'this is the minimum patent length and protection we'll accept and still innovate'. Empirical evidence on historical patent protection and investments globally remains inconclusive. It would be useful for India to have a study to figure out how well India is doing in balancing the need to attract investment with the need to keep costs low.

There are no fixed paradigms or a model on patent design which would fit the needs of all countries. While apportioning risks and ensuring R&D is adequately rewarded but not unduly so, four issues need to be kept in view:

i) Vary the length of the patent depending on the sunk cost; instead of 0–20 years, it can be 5, 8, 15 or 20 depending on costs based on credible disclosures;
ii) Assign the breadth of the patent. A more rigorous definition of

the product or a somewhat broader definition;

iii) Define which product classes would receive patent protection;

iv) Bear in mind the distinction between techniques, accidental discovery and innovations.

The design of the patent law would be critical in harmonizing the somewhat divergent interest of pricing drugs as cheaply as possible and at the same time encouraging investments in R&D. Hopefully, the debate in parliament would consider some of the economic aspects of a patent regime to bring symmetry between what economists describe as the 'Patent Theory Versus Patent Law'.

9 January 2005

37

Pension: Thinking into the Future

The panic about pensions is rising around the world. The United States, Europe, Japan, China and other countries are seeing the greying of their populations and the steady march of the demographic bulge towards pensionable age. There are attempts to stem the long-range fiscal drain by fine-tuning the basic inter-generational contracts, while other countries are revamping their systems entirely, with substantial short-term transition costs. In comparison to this scenario, India's demographics are enviable: the population is ageing, but slowly. Nearly 12 per cent of the world's ageing population lives in India (making it a potentially lucrative market for pension fund managers), but nearly 17 per cent of the world's total population also lives here.

Nevertheless, demographics are not the full story. The fiscal impact of the pension system depends on the demographics of those covered by pension plans as well as the structures of guarantees. The social benefits of having a pension system depend on its coverage. And here India looks weak. Government workers, the main group covered by pension plans, are relatively older than the general population. Their 'demographic bulge' came from hiring patterns: central government recruitment grew by 57 per cent between 1957 and 1971. The government's total liabilities are now estimated at Rs 23,629 crore (up from Rs 5,000 crore in 1995) for the centre and an additional Rs 30,000 crore for the state governments. Expenditure on central government pensions alone increased from 0.67 per cent of the GDP in 1993–94 to 1.67 per cent of the GDP (12.6 per cent of net tax revenue!) in 2003–04 even as the economy's growth speeded up.

The government also defines the interest rates for private workers' main pension options: the Public Provident Fund (PPF), the Employee's Provident Fund (EPF) and the shorter-term Post Office Monthly Income Scheme (POMIS), three options for tax-free savings with varying degrees of flexibility in contribution. Such schemes need not create a drain on public resources. In practice, however, the government-set interest rates for the funds have been higher than the government's general borrowing costs. The Special Deposit Scheme, in which the EPF is invested, for example, dropped from 9.5 to 8.5 per cent this year (with recent pressures to reverse this) but is still higher than the 6–7 per cent interest rate on which the government can otherwise borrow.

As for coverage, here too India falls short. Only thirty-five million of the 380 million labour force is covered by a pension plan. The Pension Bill solves only part of the fiscal problem and does not address the larger social issue. It introduces a newly defined contribution pension plan offering subscribers a choice of fund management options and mandates that central government civil service workers who entered service after 1 January 2004 subscribe to this plan. There is no guaranteed minimum payout, but actual payouts could be higher than under the existing scheme. The Bill also sets up the Pension Fund Regulatory and Development Authority (PFRDA) as an interim body, now likely to be put into place by ordinance after being approved by the cabinet in November 2004. Nevertheless, the Pension Bill is only a start. First, we still need a plan for working out the existing liabilities. Where will these resources come from? Second, we must take another look at the liabilities created by the EPF and the PPF. In addition to the direct drain on public resources due to the high interest rate, the tax-free savings option also distorts bank deposits and lending rates. And it is not clear that these 'subsidies' are going to the poorest—the low balances suggest that the funds are not being used to build up savings for retirement but rather as tax-saving vehicles. The new pension system offers an important improvement, but there is little incentive for workers to shift away from the tax-free, high-interest-rate accounts.

Third, simply repairing existing pension plans overlooks the fact that their coverage is limited. The remainder of the population depends on within-family, inter-generational transfers. Economic changes, however, put pressure on this traditional model. Migration has put more physical distance between generations. Urbanization has changed the way that tasks were shared. The tasks each member of the family contributes to household welfare can evolve in rural areas, but industrial jobs may not be as flexible. Longer life expectancies also increase the burden that within-family, inter-generational transfers create for children. The current life expectancy of those over sixty is now fifteen years and is expected to go up to twenty years by 2020.

From a fiscal perspective, given the many demands on public resources, it makes sense to do as much as we can to encourage private pension schemes to expand coverage. The establishment of the PFRDA is one step towards creating an attractive investment environment, but we need to make sure that it enacts and enforces credible regulation that takes into account the best practices from around the world. Opening the pension sector to foreign participation will also be a step in the right direction. Nevertheless, there will remain a need for the public sector to be involved in providing at least minimal pension for the poor and potentially, some kind of guarantee for corporate pensions.

The first challenge would be to ensure that there is minimal leakage of pension funds. A loosely targeted pension fund discourages independent savings among those who can afford to finance their own retirement and thus creates a substantial fiscal burden. India has time on its side. But time passes and the current young will age and any weaknesses now built into the system will only perpetuate. We must be careful about the commitments we make now, as they will have to be kept in the future. Reforming pension systems is near impossible when the majority of voters are beneficiaries.

The second challenge would be to make sure that the government guarantee does not encourage risky behaviour on the part of corporations. The corporations' actuarial assumptions must be carefully monitored to ensure that they match their workers' current life expectancy profile. The actuarial assumptions would preferably be regulated by an independent regulator rather than be subject to political pressure. Striking a balance between being too safe (and thus low-return) and too risky (which is potentially high-return but imposes large contingent liabilities) is a challenge for pension systems around the world. Pension reform is in the interest of 'all ages'.

Postscript

The Pensions Bill regrettably continues to await parliamentary approval. The Left parties are insisting on some critical amendments which will dilute the import of some of the key provisions. The finance minister remains optimistic that a consensus would be reached, enabling the passage of the Bill during the current session of parliament. Only time will tell.

29 December 2004

38

Banking Reforms: The Need to Walk the Talk

Just before P. Chidambaram left for the annual ritual of the World Bank and the IMF meeting in Washington, he was rather optimistic in an interview with a prestigious economic daily. This was in contrast to his somewhat guarded statement at the launch of a recent book, *India Financial Sector: Recent Reforms and Future Challenges* edited by Priya Basu, where he confessed that the lack of political consensus handicapped bold initiatives.

Financial sector reforms is one area where Chidambaram needs to 'walk the talk'. It is well recognized that financial reforms initiated in 1991–92 have not made significant progress. In overall terms, banks are much healthier, customers are better served through improved technology and development needs more responsively met. The regulatory architecture has been strengthened by the creation of SEBI for the securities markets and mutual funds and the Insurance Regulatory Development Authority for the insurance sector.

The question which we need to ask is a different one. Are we satisfied with the pace of change? Is the average Indian convinced that his cost of credit does not bear the load of inefficient financial intermediation? Is there genuine competition and dynamism in banking? Is there enough aggressiveness to meet the needs of the agriculture sector? In rural India, only Rs 2,000 crore is available against the annual credit requirement of Rs 45,000 crore. Are we enhancing the reach of the banking system in a country where 500 million individuals do not have bank accounts?

Chidambaram could not have forgotten that a roadmap on banking reforms was announced. Presumably, it includes the following:

(i) Improving the autonomy and efficiency of public sector banks; minimizing government interference and strengthening the quality of bank boards. With the exception of the Reserve Bank and the State Bank, the quality of other bank boards remains suspect. Political patronage is evident in abundance: successive governments have parked favourites on these boards. The wrongs of the past cannot be a good precedent for continuing them in future.

(ii) High-quality talent with domain knowledge cannot be attracted by the present salary structure; the dilemma of market-oriented emoluments in a 'public sector bank' needs resolution.

(iii) Strengthening accounting procedures so as to fully reflect market values of all assets in publicly disclosed statements and ensure that losses are fully revealed to shareholders, depositors and supervisors, regardless of whether they stem from Non-Performing Assets (NPAs) or higher interest rates. A bank that does not honestly report bad news will never get around to solving problems.

(iv) The uniformity of practice relating to asset classification and the adequacy of provisioning based on more truthful classification of assets are not easy. Indeed, while NPAs have significantly declined, some of the numbers remain suspect depending on how truthfully assets have been classified. The entire area of asset allocation, asset quality and capital adequacy needs to be revisited. Methodologies for risk assessment of asset quality and provisioning in the light of the perceived risk are critical for meeting Basel II norms.

(v) The high fiscal deficit is cited as a reason for all manner of conservative policies in the financial sector and monetary economics. But it does not, in any way, constrain reforms in banking that are aimed at increasing competition. If government equity in public sector banks cannot be reduced (the initiative of the NDA government to reduce equity to 33 per cent did not travel far in their own government and there is no consensus within the UPA), then the absence of competition will perpetuate inefficiency. Efforts towards consolidation, mergers and acquisition also remain stymied. It is in this context that the enhanced presence of foreign banks in India, and greater ease of entry for domestic banks can greatly help in improving the productivity and efficiency of Indian banking.

(vi) The accepted roadmap for the presence of foreign banks in India is in two phases; the first phase comprises of three components namely, foreign banks with a first-time presence who choose to operate through a branch license or set up a 100 per cent wholly owned subsidiary (WOS); existing foreign banks expanding branches through a liberal branch licensing procedure; converting existing branches to wholly owned subsidiaries or existing banks be allowed to have an equity up to 74 per cent in private Indian banks identified by the Reserve Bank for restructuring. During the last six months nothing has been heard or done on the implementation of this roadmap: either no foreign banks are eligible or they remain uninterested. This needs explanation.

(vii) A reform of the regulatory architecture by learning from the best international practice has received scant attention. Avoiding conflict of interest in regulatory institutions faces resistance which is made worse by complacency.

The roadmap for reform of the banking system has multiple objectives of which quite a few require legislative action. There are others in the regulatory or administrative domain. The last one year has seen tardy progress. Promising reforms is less than adequate; the proof of the pudding is always in the eating.

Postscript

Some key legislations still remain mired in the absence of consensus within coalition partners. These include the raise of 10 per cent cap on equity for foreign banks to reflect the structure of shareholding. Similarly the Bill to increase the equity cap from 26 per cent to 49 per cent for the insurance sector is yet to be introduced in parliament.

The opening of the banking sector to increased competition from foreign banks and also more aggressive M&As is yet to make creditable progress. While non-performing portfolios have been substantially brought down, efficiency benchmarking and a faster adoption of Basel II norms need to be carefully watched.

25 September 2005

39

Urban Reforms-Can We Stay the Course?

Just before the prime minister left for Moscow, he launched the Jawaharlal Nehru National Urban Renewal Mission. The prime minister's speech outlined the challenges of urban planning and highlighted the unresolved issues not all of which have been addressed in the Mission's statement.

An enhanced pace of urbanization is one of the inevitable outcomes of our new growth trajectory. Agriculture still provides livelihood for 68 per cent of our population while contributing 24 per cent to our GDP; sustained growth in manufacturing—coupled with the services sector—will significantly alter past trends in urbanization. An integrated approach must address regulatory and legal issues, the enforcement of existing laws, upgrading infrastructure quality, redressing problems of the urban poor including access to civic amenities, health and education. Planning for new urban centres, renewing and redeveloping existing conglomerates while addressing the concerns of metropolitan cities pose multiple challenges. So do the strains of massive temporary internal migration. This is not the first time that an urban initiative has been launched. Earlier variations include the Urban Reforms Incentive Fund, the City Challenge Fund, the Good Urban Governance Campaign, the Urban Transport Policy, the Slum Policy and the Hawkers Policy. Presumably, most of these are now amalgamated in the newly launched Urban Renewal Mission.

So what is new about this initiative? Urban reforms will now be implemented in a 'Mission mode' to cover sixty-three cities, comprising a population exceeding one million, state capitals and twenty-three other cities of religious and tourist importance. An estimated provision of Rs 50,000 crore for a period of seven years is to be made as grant-in-aid for leveraging additional resources. Access to resources will be contingent on some mandatory reforms like effective implementation of the 74th Amendment of the constitution, rationalization of stamp duty to 5 per cent over a seven-year period, repealing the Land Ceiling Act or reforming the Rent Control Act coupled with municipal reforms on accounting procedure, improving tax efficiency and the application of user charges apart from some optional measures. It will be monitored through a national committee under the minister for urban development and state-level steering committees under the chief minister.

A lot of what has been proposed is quite sensible. However, several issues cause concerns:

- First and foremost, the uncertain response of the state governments. Resources allocated under the earlier Urban Reforms Incentive Fund which had similar conditions remained underutilized. While resources have now been enhanced, is the 'carrot' attractive enough for the states to undertake some onerous reforms?
- The review of the Tenth Plan based on the Rakesh Mohan Committee estimates the annual requirement to be Rs 27,773 crore which is far in excess of even the now enhanced allocations.
- A critical factor is state-level implementation. The 74th Amendment aims at decentralization and the creation of a democratic government at local levels. It also seeks to redefine the relationship between states and municipal bodies and similarly, the need for transfer of resources to effect the recommendations of the State Finance Commission. Incentivizing state governments to do so remains a daunting challenge.
- On access to resources contingent on meeting conditionalities, the ability to leverage funds is a critical component of the programme. Will state governments create special purpose vehicles? Or organizations through which these activities are to be implemented and the borrowing undertaken on the collateral of the expected resource devolution? Predictability of resource

flow is necessary for meeting debt liabilities. Resource flows based on annual budgetary appropriations will remain uncertain. A fund that will not lapse is a budgetary aberration but makes servicing of contingent debt liabilities easier. The modalities on leveraging resources remain unclear.

- The choice between either rationalizing the rent control provisions or repealing the Urban Land Ceiling Act except in relation to activities for the poor is not rational. The objectives of improving housing for the poor and meeting their infrastructure needs are desirable and must be separately funded. The repeal of the Urban Land Ceiling Act is necessary to reduce litigation, improve supply-side response and minimize corruption in the administration of the Urban Land Ceiling Act. Rationalization of the Rent Control Act is crucial for encouraging investment in the housing sector. One is not a substitute for the other.
- The need to progressively apply user charges, contingent on assured quality of infrastructure, is vital to restore the financial health of urban local bodies. The stipulation in the Mission Statement that 'Levy of reasonable user charges with the objective that the full cost of operation and maintenance is collected within seven years' is opaque. It postpones the problem and makes implementation difficult to monitor.

Urban reforms cannot brook delay. Securing the cooperation of state governments, persuading them on the adequacy of compensation and the multiplier benefits of urban reforms are not easy. Ad hoc changes in policy, or periodically altering the nomenclature of the programme is not a substitute for difficult action. Reforms need consistency, coherence and consensus and above all, political will. Can we stay the course?

11 December 2005

40

Thought for Food

A sustained increase in farm incomes is crucial not only for growth in the GDP but also to sustain a growing market for goods and services. Integrated agricultural reforms entail cohesiveness on complex policy measures, including changes in the minimum support price (MSP) regime, a targeted public distribution system, securing improved metabolic balance in the soil by using appropriate fertilizer mixes, increased irrigation coverage through the use of rainwater harvesting, sustainable water-use techniques and effecting changes in crop patterns in consonance with changing consumer preferences and groundwater availability. Value-added agricultural activity, particularly agro-processing activity, is however central to any design for restructuring agricultural activity. Consider the following:

India, with an arable land area of 184 million hectares, produces 91 million tonnes of milk (the highest in the world), 150 million tonnes of fruits and vegetables (second highest in the world), 210 million tonnes of food grains (third highest in the world), 6.2 million tonnes of fish and has 480 million head of livestock (the highest in the world). Nonetheless, processing levels for fruits and vegetables are just 2 per cent, poultry 2.1 per cent, milk 14 per cent, and fish 4 per cent. Poor shelf life and the absence of market connectivity and outlets result in nearly 40 per cent of fruits and vegetables being wasted. In countries like Philippines and China, the processing activity is 45 per cent and 23 per cent respectively compared to our modest 7 per cent in food products.

Why has our food-processing activity not taken off?

The first reason is the absence of adequate infrastructure, particularly rural road connectivity, coupled with inadequacy of information and marketing linkages and the absence of cold chain systems. The cost of packaging (poor as it is) ranges from 10–54 per cent of the production cost. The cold chain capacity caters to less than 10 per cent of the produce and within that the facilities are so rudimentary that over 80 per cent are capable of handling only potatoes! High costs and the low availability of credit remain a problem because even within the priority sector—lending by banks for agriculture—food processing receives only 4.5 per cent of the earmarked credit.

Second, the regulatory framework which forces farmers to use designated agricultural markets to sell their produce and prevents them from directly marketing thus adding to costs and impairing flexibility. A wholesale modification of the Agricultural Produce Marketing Act and greater encouragement for contract farming are inescapable necessities. The groundwork for future policies are contained in the Food Processing Policy, 2005, prepared by the ministry for food processing. These need to be finalized. Issues of infrastructure, the adequacy of financing, legal and regulatory frameworks need to be addressed. The synchronization of the aggressive rural roads programme with mobile refrigeration facilities and linking the cold chains will minimize waste and improve farm incomes.

The most debilitating factor, however, is the legal framework. Currently, food laws span nine ministries, comprising thirteen central orders alone! In addition, states have their own control orders. Organizations responsible for enforcing these regulations are poorly staffed or trained and represent the worst vestiges of the licence permit raj. Food inspectors (a modest 4,000) are known to harass manufacturers and extract untenable rent. In 2003, the government had announced the constitution of a group of ministers to formulate an integrated food law. The composition of the group changed and so did the government. A new group under the minister for agriculture was constituted some time ago. It has completed its work expeditiously and the draft of a Food Safety and Standards Bill, 2005, has been put on the web site of the ministry for food processing. While this Bill has much to commend itself for integrating various laws into cohesive legislation and is no doubt a positive step forward, several infirmities remain. These include:

a) While everybody is conscious that the government has a social and moral obligation to promote purity in food, the Bill seeks to achieve this by excessive controls through elaborate licensing procedures. The Bill is clearly draconian and gives power to food inspectors under Section 38 to inspect, search and seize and the offences are punishable with imprisonment. These powers are liable to be misused given the mindset of the food inspectors. We need to consider whether, instead of licensing, we can de-license the sector, prescribe food standards rigorously and impose heavy financial penalties for deviation from prescribed standards. Creating a vast network of food inspectors may not be the most efficient means to achieve the broad objective shared by all of 'ensuring availability of safe and wholesome food for human consumption'.
b) There is little evidence to suggest that the new authority will have autonomy. The composition of the authority, under Section 5 of the Bill, consisting of several joint secretaries of various ministries, their selection through a committee headed by the cabinet secretary, the procedures for their removal, the inherent powers retained by the government to issue directives over a wide range of issues do not inspire confidence either in its independent constitution or functioning.
c) In fact, Article 8(C) of the proposed Act on dealing with the removal of members is liable to ambiguous interpretation. So is the unusual proviso on the possibility of the authority itself being superceded. We have rarely heard of authorities or regulators being superceded, except through new legislation. Both the members of the authority and indeed, the authority itself are thus vulnerable to the political exigencies of the time.
d) Curiously, the Act does not stipulate the administrative ministry under the aegis of which the proposed authority would be constituted. If the focus is development instead of regulation, the

ministry of food processing would be its logical home. The mandate of the ministry of food processing needs clarification for ensuring coordination of post-harvest activity, which is currently dispersed over a number of institutions.

A lot of time and effort has gone into the drafting of this Bill. Sharad Pawar deserves credit for completing a difficult task quickly. However, if this Bill is to truly meet international benchmarks, it needs to be divested of the subsisting license-permit-raj mindset. The powers prescribed under the Act, methods of appointment, removal and enforcement need to be simplified. After all, the end objective is to make it easier, simpler, safer and more profitable for the agro-processing industry to come up in this country. A draconian law in the offing may not be the best means to achieve this end. We need food for thought.

Postscript

The implementation of the Food Processing Policy remains mired in the turf battle on the ownership of regulations. Both the ministries of food processing and health continue to vie that the subject lies in their domain. The result is that a regulator has yet to be appointed and the implementation of the Act remains stalled.

23 January 2005

41

Getting Projects on Track

The recent regional meeting of the Confederation of Indian Industry (CII) had 'Sustainable Competitive Growth: Are We On Track' as its theme. The panelists included Yogi Deveshwar, Surjit Bhalla, Dilip Kapuria, Suhel Seth, Laila Tyabji, Jose Salinas from Mexico and myself. On the substantive issue, the panelists and more so the participants seemed to broadly agree that we are 'on track', but much needs to be done to consolidate current gains and shoot for a 10 per cent GDP growth.

The challenges were familiar: improve infrastructure, pay greater attention to education and particularly to making the literate employable, improve governance in weaker states and forge understanding among political parties on some common issues. Remaining competitive means adaptating to changing market requirements; societies which actively foster an 'innovative culture' have obvious advantages. While global outsourcing is a profitable business, our competitive edge can be eroded if inadequate supply of skilled labour pushes up wage rates significantly. Of course it would be naive to assume that the 8 per cent growth rate is in our pocket and the struggle now is to achieve the goal of 10 per cent growth rate set by the prime minister. There are the more conservative estimates of a 5.5–6 per cent growth outlined by Shankar Acharya in the concluding paragraph of his recent book *Essays on Macroeconomic Policy and Growth in India*, cautioning us with a quotation from George Eliot that, 'among all forms of mistake, prophecy is the most gratuitous'. There is also a lengthy critique contained in T.N. Srinivasan's recent essay 'Status of Indian Economic Reforms: A Hiatus or a Pause Before Acceleration?' These sobering analyses caution against excessive exuberance and although it can be credibly argued that while we may well be on the way to 7 per cent growth, getting to 10 per cent will be a whole new ball game.

Let me however concentrate on a somewhat different aspect of growth strategy. Shekhar Gupta, who was the moderator of the panel discussion, asked me pointedly why things took so long in the government. He, for instance, mentioned that a proposal for a Rs 100-crore grant to the Indian Science Institute announced in last year's budget had only been recently submitted to the cabinet. Besides, work on several road projects for which contracts were awarded last June was yet to begin. The issues raised by him are significant.

The first problem is the lack of accountability. Civil servants have rarely been penalized for delayed decisions and are never rewarded for accelerated action. Cautious and sometimes even tardy decisions that guarantee job security and career progression are the preferred option. The complex web of accountability acts as a further dampener to accelerated public service. Transferring attitudes and procedures from the private sector to public delivery systems is not easy. The answer may lie in more aggressive outsourcing to the private sector and the lateral induction of talent within the hierarchy. Hopefully, the new authority currently being discussed as part of the civil service reform package will address these concerns.

Second, new initiatives announced in the budget are sometimes knee-jerk reactions. Finance ministers soften the blow of some unpopular decisions by announcing a whole slew of initiatives to present what they believe are 'more balanced proposals'. In practice, this means that the first time ministries hear of a proposal may be just before the budget and at any rate it gives them inadequate time to prepare detailed proposals, discuss things with all stakeholders and secure requisite approvals for work to commence soon after the passage of the finance Bill. While surprise announcements lend some mystique to the budget, in practice, they can greatly delay implementation. If the public sees no visible progress after months, even years after a budget announcement has been made, it grows cynical.

Third, the procedures for project approvals or financial rules relating to disbursement, including the treasury code followed by state governments, remain anachronistic. While in substance these are designed to prevent the misuse of public funds, whenever an individual aberration has come to notice, only a new set of riders covering the generality of cases has been added. Public funds garnered through taxes must be spent with caution, care and prudential norms. However, if the underlining approach is resource conservation, with the discouragement of disbursements and the fear of future objections from supervisory agencies, delayed implementation is inevitable.

The recently constituted administrative reforms commission should suggest a model treasury code and financial rules, particularly for state governments, which combine the virtues of prudential norms with speedier implementation.

Fourth, while accountability is desirable, excessive supervision can be debilitating. The joke among field officers, including bank officials, is to avoid the three Cs—Comptroller and Auditor General, the Central Vigilance Commission and the Central Bureau of Investigation—which is suggestive of an anxious mindset. Therefore, caution instead of development becomes the central objective. The bleak prospect of a rapidly shrinking government necessitates vastly improved efficiency in the public delivery system. States which have lagged behind will be in continual need of public investments before private entrepreneurs find the climate favourable. Besides, 'reforms with a human face' will imply the enhanced role of public agencies in education, health, rural development and employment to name a few. Time and cost overruns in public projects have been debated for long. It has remained difficult to assign responsibility. Land acquisition, environmental clearance, recalcitrant contractors, pending litigation and delayed resource assignment deflect blame to faceless institutions, obviating individual liability. We must disentangle malfeasance from incompetence. Putting projects on track is central to our growth strategy.

Postscript

Tardy implementation of projects continues to be worrisome. This is particularly so when public outlays have substantially increased in the last two fiscal years. An outlay outcome statement, along with a performance profile, presents progress in physical and financial terms. However, the quality of public expenditure and the extent to which the intended project objective has been met remain debatable. The shortfall in Plan expenditure in the current year even in the flagship programme of the National Rural Employment Guarantee Schemes reflects the need to improve the efficacy and efficiency of public delivery systems. The tardy progress of the National Highways Development Roads programme and other components of the Bharat Nirman Programme also deserve priority attention.

The interim recommendations of the administrative reforms commission do not include a revised model treasury code and financial rules.

9 April 2006

42

Getting Cross with Cross-Subsidies

This is the season when it is fashionable for all and sundry to give unsolicited advice to P. Chidambaram. Finance ministers are tolerant, fully conscious that the basic budget story involves multiple inflexibilities. The arithmetic of accounting limits manoeuvrability. During the winter session of the parliament, Chidamabram presented, for the second time, a White Paper on subsidies to promote discussion and share concerns on multiple hidden and explicit subsidies. Subsidy discussions have primarily centred around the public distribution system, the application of user charges for public utilities and the pricing of farm inputs. Subsidy targeting has also been discussed with little tangible outcomes.

India is replete with cross-subsidies where one sector or segment bears an extra cost for a subsidy within the segment. To say the least, the cost of such cross-subsidies is neither carefully calculated nor explicitly known and yet cross-subsidies span large segments of economic activity:

- Railways: Overcharging on freights to subsidize passenger traffic. Within the freight segment itself, uneconomic freight subsidizes other categories of goods and there are differential subsidies between various classes of passengers.
- Petroleum: The well-known subsidy is by overcharging petrol to subsidize kerosene and LPG. Diesel prices fluctuate sometimes on and sometimes not on par with import parity price.

- Civil Aviation: Passengers on economic routes being penalized to pay for connectivity to uneconomic routes and the more profit-making airports subsidizing the loss-making airports.
- Telecom: The Universal Service Obligation and the Access Deficit Charge cast a burden on existing consumers, particularly long distance and international callers, for enabling rural connectivity.
- Electricity: Surcharges which penalize domestic and industrial consumers to pay for either free electricity or electricty provided at less than economic cost to certain categories of users.

The list is long. Cross-subsidies are convenient for finance ministers. In the event of their elimination, if social and equity considerations necessitate their continuation, the budget will have to directly bear their burden. The ever-present fiscal compulsion makes this difficult. Continuation of such subsidies is therefore a convenient option. This masks the real incidence of fiscal distortion. Cross-subsidies may be appealing on equity considerations by making the rich pay for the poor. It is a kind of redistribution within sectors, but is it the most efficient way to effect redistribution?

It is not for at least three reasons:

First, if we are going to have cross-subsidies, we should carefully consider who is subsidizing whom and what is the effect of 'tax' in a broader context. Cross-subsidies as implemented in India do not generally redistribute from the rich to the poor. Electricity cross-subsidies, for example, are not means-tested for the wealthier consumers pay more. They are instead subsidies to the non-commercial users borne by the commercial users. These industries are not necessarily 'rich', and handicapping them only hurts the poor in the longer run by making investment in industry less attractive and reducing the number of jobs that are created. On the other hand, extracting higher prices more directly from wealthier people has a lesser effect: additional taxes placed on the rich might reduce their current available income, but the elasticity of investment to income is probably less than one. They will go ahead and invest the same amount, or nearly the same amount, in creating jobs for the economy.

The advantages of means-tested cross-subsidies over the current rough industry-household method depend on the relative sizes of two effects: the 'substitution effect' and the 'wealth effect'. When industry is taxed, investment in Indian industry becomes less attractive, so entrepreneurs look elsewhere, such as other countries, or other forms of investment. This is a 'substitution effect'. When rich people are taxed, investment is likely to be only slightly lower because while their overall pool of funds shrinks, their investment in industry stays more or less the same. This is the (loosely speaking) 'wealth effect'!

I argue that the 'wealth effect' is smaller than the 'substitution effect' for two reasons: (i) The substitution effect is significant: the market for attracting investment is global and pretty competitive. A small disadvantage is all it takes for Indian industry to lose a lot of investment. (ii) Wealth effect is small: the marginal utility of consumption is pretty low for rich people—there is a general consensus that consumption displays decreasing marginal utility and they are already consuming plenty. The marginal utility of investment, however, is not necessarily decreasing for an individual. So when their pool of discretionary income drops and they have the choice of cutting investment or cutting consumption, they cut the one that affects their marginal utility less—which would be consumption. So investment may even stay the same.

Second, cross-subsidies are more distortionary than broader redistribution through the general government budget. They change the relative costs of the consumption of various goods, leading people (especially the beneficiaries) to change their behaviour and consume more of whatever is being subsidized than they would otherwise. Why not simply tax the population that is now subsidizing services directly and give a 'living grant' to poorer people that would cover a certain normatively desirable level of electricity, water, rail transport, etc.; price these things at market or cost-recovering levels for everyone and let people spend their grant on these services as they see fit. The beneficiaries might well be happier—they have more freedom to choose what to spend on, and the subsidizers would be no worse off than before. Of course, as argued above, the pool of subsidizers would be changed too. But the main point is that broad-based redistribution is a 'pareto improvement' over sector-specific redistribution—it makes some people better off, while making no person worse off.

Third, cross-subsidies are a nightmare when considering public–

private participation. Whatever their merits for completely government-run services, they make it really difficult to the kind of firm-specific accounting required for private participation. While the government might care only if the sector as a whole is making money, the private company cares if it is making money. Cross-subsidies are incompatible with the kinds of public–private partnerships that India is moving towards, both in rhetoric and in fact.

Chidambaram cannot be expected to do all things in one go. I also doubt the progress he can make on many of his 'loud thinking' proposals contained in the White Paper on subsidies. Subsidies may in some cases be justified on social and equity considerations if targeted sensibly. However, cross-subsidies are distortionary to the economy, irrational in conception and clumsy in implementation. They deserve a 'sunset clause' even if outright abolition is not feasible. The least we can expect from Chidambaram is a commitment to progressively eliminate these irrationalities. No expenditure management policy can be oblivious to these concerns. Coalition politics is no excuse to overlook these endemic and long-pending corrections. It is difficult to avoid not getting 'cross with cross subsidies'.

6 February 2005

43

Time to Repeal Small Cess Acts

Some time ago, I made some suggestions for reforming the ministry of finance. These included repealing laws which have outlived their utility. All tax-related legislations must be rational and serve the needs of the time. One area on which there is persistent ambiguity is cess.

While a precise definition of cess is somewhat elusive, Jas Bains says that 'in modern terms, cess is used to describe a tax on a tax. This meaning has been derived from Irish farmers, as those who have the most successful yield pay the most tax on their crop to the Government (cess for assess).' In the Indian context, however, the Supreme Court, in a ruling in Shinde Brothers versus Commissioner, Raichur reported in 1967, said that 'the word cess means a tax and is generally used when the levy is for some special administrative expense', citing various examples suggesting the name of the cess explains the object.

The cess on petrol and diesel which finances the National Highway Development Programme as well as rural roads is understandable and is directly earmarked for its end use. In fact, its proceeds go to a corpus which enables market borrowing based on securitization of the anticipated revenue stream. Similarly, the education cess recently imposed is designed to augment resources for enabling us to meet the necessary but somewhat daunting targets for human resource development. While the cess for NHDP and education are recent and their use understandable, there are many small cesses being collected through a number of legislations which we have all forgotten.

Here is a list of small cesses being collected by a multitude of laws in 2003–04:

- Cess on bidis: The Bidis Workers' Welfare Act, 1976; amount collected: Rs 94.05 crores.
- Cess on iron ore: iron ore mines, manganese ore mines and chrome; the Mines Labour Welfare Cess Act, 1976; amount collected: Rs 7.72 crores.
- Cess on limestone and dolomite: The Limestone and Mines Labour Welfare Fund Act, 1972; amount collected: Rs 16.49 crores.
- Cess on feature films: The Cine Workers Welfare Cess Act, 1981; amount collected: Rs 90.36 lakhs.

Objective: The above four welfare funds are to be administered by the ministry of labour to provide housing, medical care, educational and recreational facilities to workers employed in the bidi industry, certain non-coal mines and cine workers.

- Cess on coal and coke: Coal Mines (Conservation and Development) Act, 1974. Objective: provision for conservation and safety measures in the coal mines and the development of road and rail transport infrastructure in the coal mine areas. Amount Collected: Rs 230 crores.
- Cess on Copra: Copra Cess Act, 1979. Objective: An Act to provide the imposition of cess on Copra for the development of the coconut industry and for matters connected therewith. Amount collected: Rs 9,000.
- Cess on coffee: Coffee Act, 1942. Objective: Coffee board implements various plan schemes for development of coffee under which various types of financial/ technical assistance are provided to coffee growers. Amount collected: Rs 50,000.
- Cess on oil and oil seeds: Produce Cess Act, 1966. Amount collected: Rs 46, 87,000.
- Cess on vegetable oil: Ministry of Agriculture (Department of Agriculture) Notification No. G.S.R. 882 (E), dated 8-12-1983. Amount collected: Rs 17, 80,000.

- Cess on jute: Jute Manufacturers Cess Act, 1983. Objective: For the purpose of carrying out measures for the development of jute manufacturers and for matters connected therewith. Amount collected: Rs 40.37 crores.
- Cess on rubber: Rubber Act, 1947. Objective: To set a minimum price for rubber growers so as to stabilize rubber prices. Amount collected: Rs 84.16 crores.
- Cess on salt: Salt Cess Act, 1953. Objective: Raising funds to meet the expenses incurred on the salt organization maintained by the government and on the measures taken by government in connection with the manufacture, supply and distribution of salt. Amount collected: Rs 2.77 crores.
- Cess on sugar: Sugar Cess Act, 1982. Objective: The imposition of a cess on sugar for the development of the sugar industry and for matters connected therewith. Amount collected: Rs 341.57 crores.
- Cess on tea: Tea Act, 1953. Objective: Cess levied on tea goes to the Tea Board. Amount collected: Rs 26.86 crores.
- Cess on cotton: Produce Cess Act, 1966. Objective: The proceeds of the cess are utilized to meet the expenditure incurred in connection with measures to promote the improvement, development and marketing of produce under the Act, which includes cotton. Amount collected: Rs 4,22,000.
- Cess on textiles: Objective: To promote development of textiles, woollen fabrics, art silk fabrics and man-made fabric. Amount collected: Rs 41.61 crores.
- Handloom cess on rayon and artsilk fabric: Textile Committee Act, 1963. Amount collected: Rs 3,000.
- Handloom cess on woolen fabrics: Amount collected: Rs 22,000.
- Handloom cess on cotton fabrics: Amount collected: Rs 9,12,99,000
- Handloom cess on man-made fabrics: Amount collected: Rs 54,000
- Cess on tobacco: Tobacco Cess Act, 1975. Objective: Cess collected under this Act goes to the Tobacco Board. Amount collected: Rs 13,94,000.
- Cess on paper: Industries (Development and Regulation) Act, 1951. Amount collected: Rs 18.39 crores.
- Cess on straw board: Amount collected: Rs 13,87,000. Objective:

To promote the straw board industry.

- Cess on automobiles: Objective: To promote the automobile sector. Amount collected: Rs 77.19 crores
- Cess on matches: Amount collected: Rs 37,000.
- Cess on other commodities: Amount collected: Rs 2,77,000.

The above twenty-six cesses administered under twenty-seven Acts yield a princely sum of Rs 993 crores. In fact, the cess on copra yields Rs 9,000 while handloom cess on rayon and artsilk fabric yields Rs 3,000. The cost of keeping records, both of their realization and their expenditure, would in many cases exceed the amount collected from the cess. Clearly, their continuation and the enabling legislations have ceased to be relevant. Their repeal will clear up the books with little revenue consequence. The finance ministry should coordinate with administrative ministries for getting them repealed in the budget session. Continuing with the cesspool of cesses whose collection and use we have forgotten does not contribute to public good.

18 September 2005

VIII

POLITICAL DYNAMICS

44

Going beyond Good Intentions

Manmohan Singh respects authority, he is its repository, but is certainly not authoritarian. Carrying out reforms in governance has been his recurring theme. These reforms include administrative reforms at the centre and the states including field administration. However, only time will tell whether action will match intention. Despite all this, not everyone in the government feels the same way. Take the following four cases:

First, the proposed amendment to the Indian Medical Council Act, 1956. This Act is designed to be modified by the Indian Medical Council Amendment Bill, 2005, which confers draconian powers on the government. Nobody believes that the Council is free from partison politics and other irregularities. The rectitude of some of its members may be suspect but there are provisions in the existing Act itself and other enabling laws to deal with individual aberrations.

Consider some proposed changes:

(i) In case a nominated member fails to withdraw from the council, 'the Central Government may give such direction and if the member refuses to comply with the direction so given, it may, by order, remove such a member from the council.' So much for the independence of members.

(ii) In discharging its functions, the council should be guided by such directions as may be given in the public interest by the central government and furthermore, 'whether a question relates to public interest or not, the decision of the Central Government thereon shall be final.' So, wherever inconvenient, government issues a directive with impunity and it does not matter if council autonomy is the casualty.

(iii) 'The Central Government can dissolve the executive committee or remove from office the president or the vice president as the case may be.' So the sword of Damocles constantly hangs on the key members.

(iv) Upon the enactment of these amendments, the existing council shall stand dissolved and the central government can appoint a board of administrators to run the affairs till elections to the council are held.

These changes undercut the autonomy of the council. They confer excessive powers on the administrative ministry, creating opportunities for political patronage.

Second, telecom is one area where reforms have succeeded. The deregulation has increased tele-density, lowered costs and made India a competitive destination. Consumers have benefited; voice and data connectivity is more reliable at a significantly lower cost. The Telecom Regulatory Act defines the orbit of influence of the government, the regulator and its appellate authority. The revised Section 25 of the Act enables policy directives to be issued but was designed to be used sparingly.

In several areas, the role of the Telecom Regulatory Authority of India (TRAI) is advisory, although the government is obligated to seek its advice. In others, its advice is mandatory and also binding on the government. The ministry is now in conflict with the TRAI on issues of tariff, access deficit charge and advice pertaining to spectrum policy. Some of these are in the regulator's domain; policy directives to dilute regulatory functions do not augur well.

Third, power sector reforms have clearly slowed down. The culture of providing free power is back with a vengeance as is borne out by Amarinder Singh's free power gesture in Punjab. This has complicated lives for other states, creating uncertainties in the future of user charges. The Central Electricity Act, 2003, came under pressure from the Left parties on issues relating to unbundling of State Electricity

Boards (SEBs), rural electrification, review of the elimination of cross-subsidies and extending the date for the reorganization of the SEBs. These need to be resolved in dialogue with the UPA partners and through enabling administrative action obviating the need to amend the Act itself. Using this opportunity to erode the regulator's power by stipulating that the Electricity Regulatory Commission 'shall act in conformity' instead of the present 'shall be guided' by the National Electricity Policy is a significant dilution of regulatory functions.

It is reported that the PMO has turned down the power ministry's suggestions; the ministry of finance and the Planning Commission also have conflicting points of view. All this comes at a time when the design of the tariff policy and the methodology governing its architecture, as well as assigning responsibility between the regulator and the ministry, remain unresolved. They add to investor uncertainty.

Finally, the proposal to induct political appointees to the boards of PSUs is retrograde. It cuts at the root of granting greater autonomy to public sector undertakings. The petroleum ministry may have partially resiled in its decision to foist additional government and political appointees on boards but reports about the department of public enterprises looking up old circulars to achieve these ends is hardly endearing.

It is true that a coalition government reduces prime ministerial control on ministers representing coalition parties but the principle of collective responsibility is indivisible. The zest for improved governance cannot coexist with erosion of regulatory bodies, established institutions and public undertakings. No one knows better than the prime minister that good governance must go beyond good intentions.

2 October 2005

45

Seeking Independence from the Politics of Divisiveness

Independence Day speeches have now settled into a fixed mould which is difficult to shake off. However, the prime minister, in his Independence Day speech, has spared us new announcements which foist an unwelcome burden on the already overstretched slew of populist measures. He concentrated on the basics: presenting a report card on the recent economic success, particularly continued economic growth and the need to create employment, mitigate growing income and regional divides, ameliorate the woes of farmers and spur faster growth. He also equally stressed our growing security concerns—cross-border terrorism and the Naxalite movement—which need better intelligence, policing and socio-economic measures.

The president's speech was somewhat unusual because it concentrated on 'Case Studies', namely, success stories of voluntary initiatives on agriculture, education, health care and rural development. The prime minister promised the launch of a mission on vocational education to address our skill deficit. This does not come a day late. He ended his address by urging political leaders to think deeply and to 'shun the politics of divisiveness and adopt the policies of change and progress.' He also stressed that 'our political parties and leaders must learn to work together to build a consensus around national issues'.

Similarly, the president also said that he would be suggesting to the government and both houses of parliament 'to formulate a Citizen Security Bill (National Campaign for Eradication of Terrorism), formulate an Energy Independence Bill and adopt a resolution that India will be transformed into an economically developed nation before 2020'. Both the prime minister and the president clearly believe the need for sustained bipartisan support to address our major developmental challenges. Coalition politics often results in even small allies holding governments to ransom. Regional and fringe parties drive the national agenda. The lack of trust between mainstream parties gives regional parties a disproportionate say in national decision making. This is neither reflective of a national consensus nor does it augur well for continuity of policies. Governments in office invariably see the principal opposition party as uncooperative. At the same time they are embarrassed to seek its support lest their moves be misunderstood by their partners. This makes the emergence of consensus even more difficult. Nonetheless, there is no alternative. So the question now is: What should be the key ingredients of a national concordance?

First, the two foremost areas are foreign policy and defence. For long, non-alignment has been the bedrock of our foreign policy. In a vastly different world, strategic partnership with other major developed countries, particularly the United States, is an inescapable reality. The nuclear deal, which should have been a unifying ingredient considering the multiple advantages it confers and the approval process in the US government, is clearly not to be blamed for the divisiveness introduced in what was hitherto an area of continuity.

Second, depoliticizing public delivery systems: Monitoring of outcomes or increased public investment, particularly in rural areas through the National Rural Employment Guarantee Scheme or Bharat Nirman, cannot be meaningful if the delivery system remains clogged with incessant political interference. Can there be consensus among parties on some accepted 'rules of the game', which would partially free public delivery systems from discretionary political decision making?

Third, public expenditure: There should be some consensus on areas where public expenditure would be justified. Evaluation of expenditure outcomes, more importantly the efficacy of subsidies and the impact on intended beneficiaries, is inescapable.

Fourth, there should be a balance between development initiatives and their consequences, mainly resettlement and rehabilitation. While some displacement and transitional difficulties may be inevitable, what would be the appropriate benchmarks for assessing the adequacy of compensation and apportioning of benefits?

Fifth, energy security, not only in exploring alternative energy forms, economizing its usage and concerted action on both demand and supply but also the pricing of energy among different users and the reasonableness of subsidized energy activity, needs rational review.

Sixth, to make educational systems inclusive yet not lose sight of merit and enhance capacities to leverage the advantages of a young demographic profile needs coherent and actionable milestones.

Finally, key legislations need to be implemented quicker. Legislations in general will always be political, involving negotiations between different actors, but there are some which are so compelling in our broader economic interest that tardy action is clearly unreasonable.

46

Why We Need a Core Economic Agenda

The recent cabinet decision to remove the 10 per cent cap on voting rights on foreign banks has evoked favourable responses all around. Its rationale is simple—no sensible investor will put up money unless voting rights reflect the corpus committed. This decision is an integral part of the banking reform road map now approved by the government. The euphoria generated in banking circles may, however, be somewhat premature.

- The decision fulfilled a promise made a year ago. Chidambaram's first budget speech of 8 July 2004 contained this commitment.
- While this decision marks the latest implementation of commitments made at that time, one important unfulfilled promise remains: to raise the cap on foreign equity for insurance from 26 per cent to 49 per cent. We have heard nothing recently about the insurance matter but presumably even minimum consensus within the UPA eludes a formal cabinet decision for enabling introduction of a Bill to amend the earlier act.
- The fate of the decision is still uncertain. The amendment of the Banking Regulation Act containing the voting rights provision is likely to be referred to the standing committee. This is not the first time such a Bill has been introduced. An earlier version by the NDA government went to the standing committee but was allowed to lapse.

The present bill is a refinement of the earlier bill since any acquisition beyond 5 per cent now requires RBI approval (this is considered a prudential requirement and could lend some comfort to Left-oriented detractors) whereas the earlier one was based on an automatic approval. The Left parties have vehemently opposed the new bill and the BJP has also made negative remarks. If both the Left parties and the BJP oppose the bill, its passage in parliament is guaranteed to fail. Either the Left reconciles, believing that the new safeguards are adequate to allay misgivings, or the BJP change their mind.

The present state of play raises the more important issue that a basic distrust between the two mainstream parties makes pursuit of economic reforms an uphill task. Governments, when in power, think differently from how they did when they were in the opposition. Economic development becomes a casualty in the tactical manoeuvres of political dynamics.

Take the case of the Congress first. While in opposition, it gave NDA a hard time when it asked them for their consent to open up the insurance sector. The present limit of 26 per cent on foreign investment was the outcome of prolonged negotiations. On banking reforms, the bill introduced by a former finance minister to reduce government equity to 33 per cent in nationalized banks which would have brought about a culture change, even while retaining its public sector character, did not receive any support from the Congress. Informal interlocutors from the NDA to persuade the Congress drew a blank. Proposed changes in labour laws faced a similar fate. However, there were several other important bills like the Electricity Bill, 2003, and the changes in telecom policy, to name a few, which did receive their support and became law.

Reversing roles when the UPA came to power, it is curious that measures actively pursued by the BJP like the introduction of VAT, raising foreign equity in insurance from 26 per cent to 49 per cent, increasing the cap on voting rights beyond 10 per cent, are now being opposed by the NDA. The opposition to the introduction of VAT is the worst case because even though this may have been conceived by an earlier Congress government, it was actively pursued by two successive NDA finance ministers. The detection of loopholes overnight when the NDA moved to the opposition is inexplicable.

The development process requires continuity of policies. Spokesmen for successive governments marketing India as a credible investment destination have argued that changes in India are embedded in a deeper social consensus which spans political parties. Further, that seven successive governments since 1991 have pursued the same set of policies while altering priorities, sequencing and nuancing them to suit their needs.

Given the federal nature of our polity, where coalition politics is the likely pattern in the foreseeable future and several demographically large states will be governed by regional parties, policy consistency is central to any development strategy. It is now well accepted that in any fractured coalition politics, regional parties or coalition partners will drive the national agenda in the absence of minimum understanding between two mainstream national parties. It is a challenge to the ingenuity of senior political leadership in both these parties to devise a workable strategy so that policies discussed for long and broadly endorsed do not become the casualty of short-term political gains.

The number of important legislations which were either not introduced following opposition even prior to the bill securing cabinet approval, or worse, allowed to lapse in either of the houses or the standing committee is quite large.

The national Common Minimum Programme is a common agenda of the UPA partners. So is the manifesto of the NDA representing a broad commonality between the NDA partners. Evolving a 'core agenda' on some key issues like legislations to govern a regulatory framework for infrastructure, social security system, reform of banking and financial institutions, improving the supervisory and prudential standards to protect small shareholders and investors, improving productivity of coal for power needs or enhancing the efficiency of ports, freeing agriculture from a cluster of outdated regulations or making mega cities and urban conglomerations more livable or improving education and health efficiency are some areas where commonalities should be higher than divisiveness.

A common core agenda must span the political spectrum. Who should take the initiative? Policy initiatives are usually the prerogative of the government in office. The corpus of legislative and regulatory changes which await us is an enormous challenge. Getting a bill or two through ploy or clever floor management speaks well of the incumbents but in the long run is no substitute to consensus-based broad commonalities.

The present stalemate in parliament can only be a transient aberration. This is only the first year of the government and national elections are not on the horizon. India's interest is far too important to be blighted by tactical political ploys on who should take credit and on whom the blame must rest.

16 May 2005

47

The New 'Consensus Mantra'

The Confederation of Indian Industry (CII) has just concluded its National Conference 2006. New office bearers have taken charge and will inevitably set their own priorities within the framework of continuity which this organization has come to represent. Yogi Deveshwar's credible record in improving governance within the CII and increased decentralization represents an important contribution. Over the years, CII has evolved. It has moved away from being a mere 'industry spokesman' to engage on broader issues of economic and social policies. Its overseas network has begun to leverage the advantages of a growing Indian market for promoting our strategic and foreign policy interests. The negotiating dexterity and fabled global networking of its chief mentor, Tarun Das, has lent credence to these initiatives. Its dialogue with state governments and engagement on issues like health, education, women empowerment and decentralization to local bodies is a far cry from excessive preoccupation with tax reduction, delicensing and protection to Indian industry. CII's new agenda mirrors the concerns of a new India.

Prime ministers have in the past used the annual conference to unveil new packages to enthuse the corporate world. Promises on tax reform, public expenditure initiatives like the Golden Quadrilateral, reforming the infrastructure or deregulating telecom were some major announcements earlier. This year was somewhat different. The prime minister did stress the need to increase the share of the manufacturing sector in national income and to implement the worthwhile recommendations of the National Competitive Council through a high-level committee under his chairmanship, apart from stressing the virtues of a 'cluster approach' to secure economies of scale, particularly through the special economic zones and further strengthening our capabilities in information technology. All this is either known or is not exciting enough to make headlines. What has attracted attention is his suggestion for 'industry to seriously consider enhancing educational and employment opportunities for weaker sections, investing in their skill enhancement and promoting their employment in an affirmative manner as well as to invest more in vocational training and technical education, particularly for youth from less privileged background.' He went on to suggest that to 'assess at a firm level, the diversity in your employee profile and commit yourself voluntarily to making it more broad-based and representative. Such affirmative action can be a crucial component of an inclusive society we hope to build.'

The prime minister's suggestions to industry has evoked a mixed response. Many view this as a move away from a merit-based system which enhances quality and retains our competitiveness. Others view voluntary action as being preferable to a formal legislation. While the prime minister has certainly triggered a fresh debate he has also tried to fend off pressures within his cabinet for more draconian measures like a new law, if need be through a constitutional amendment. The controversy about quota reservation in the private sector comes immediately after the controversial proposal of the HRD minister for extending reservations even in centres of excellence to OBCs, effectively foreclosing 49 per cent of all admissions. The two issues taken together does represent a move away from 'meritocracy' to 'social empowerment'. The economic virtues of meritocracy are obvious enough. India's comparative factor advantage lies in the availability of skilled manpower at a competitive cost and the sustenance of productivity and efficiency gains. While supply side elasticity gives room for manoeuvre, a socially mandated quota could seriously undercut the newly discovered opportunities which IT and knowledge-based activity confer on us. On the other hand, bringing the disadvantaged into the mainstream is critical for social cohesiveness and political stability as a precondition for long-term growth. Combining the virtues of meritocracy with social empowerment is never easy and alternative options must be evaluated more carefully. On a different note, the prime minister, in the award ceremony of the *Indian Express*, in which he gave away prizes to sixteen leading journalists in the previous week, had drawn a distinction between debate and a discussion: the former brings to the fore opposite points of view while the latter attempts to reconcile and forges consensus. While advising the industry for voluntary affirmative action and leaving space for greater consultations on quota reservations in educational institutions, the prime minister is seeking a new consensus. However, any consensus strategy must distinguish between issues which are innately divisive as compared to issues which are contentious. Socially divisive issues need attitudinal reconciliation inherited from history and will remain controversial for long. On the other hand, contentious issues have greater prospect of achieving convergence of divergent points of view.

Since it would be better to seek consensus on contentious issues, we must focus on those where long-term multiplier benefits are obvious and easier to explain. These would inevitably include a more flexible labour market to give impetus for new employment; rationalizing subsidies where it can genuinely benefit the poor; rationalizing user charges of public utilities, including municipal entities, for incentivizing fresh investment; enacting critical legislation in infrastructure like coal and ports or improving the efficiency of financial intermediation through greater competition which makes it easier for the ordinary man to borrow at more affordable costs; and redesigning the agricultural strategy in consonance with changing consumer needs and sustainable cultivation patterns and reforming the education system to harness the advantages of a young demographic profile.

Socially divisive issues require much wider debate over a longer period and taking hurried action for perceived short-term electoral gains would exasperate the social divide and deflect attention from our growth challenges.

The 'consensus mantra' must be applied differentially. It should not be a device for leadership to postpone decisions. The strategy must begin to harvest some early gains. Resolving contentious issues cannot be postponed if the lofty aim of 10 per cent growth rate is to be realized. Differentiated action and approach are what enlightened leadership is all about.

23 April 2006

48

When Report Cards Are Ready Reckoners

This has been a week full of report cards and agitations. The completion of the UPA government's two years triggered independent surveys rating its performance even while the government put out a list of its laudable achievements. Many of these are ongoing activities which do not deserve any special mention. The quota agitation, to say the least, is distracting and has reopened old wounds in bringing out the inherent divisiveness of the polity. Hopefully, a middle consensus ground would find acceptance before investors enhance their risk perceptions. Add to this the growing Naxalite violence covering 165 districts out of 602. Risk perceptions are always difficult to quantify and even while brave economists impute numbers, they have an intangible quality which shapes our decisions. So how has the government performed in the last two years? The prime minister has hesitated in writing any scorecard. A perceived decline in his standing in the survey conducted by the *Hindustan Times* was contrary to the outcome of the NDTV survey. *India Today* assigned marks to individual ministers, benchmarking them against last year's rating, 'based on popular perceptions'.

First and foremost, since we do not have a foreign minister, success in the area of foreign policy does not figure in these surveys and yet improving relations with countries in Asia, profiting from a closer integration with these economies, improved relations with China and persevering with peace initiatives with Pakistan are no mean achievements. Above all, the Congressional approval on civil nuclear arrangements with the US, enabling access to civil nuclear energy and dual technology with strategic partnership, invests the future with multiplier benefits. This would be the UPA government's single biggest achievement. It augurs well for enhanced FDI flows from the US and Japan, provided there is no deterioration in the domestic environment and infrastructure improves rapidly.

Second, on the economic front, there are no comparable gains. P. Chidambaram can draw comfort from withstanding pressures of fiscal profligacy or reversing tax reform and securing universal acceptance of VAT. But reforms of the financial sector, pension and insurance as well as liberalization of FDI flows remain mired in coalition politics. While he still remains the most acceptable reform face of the government, it is not surprising that in the *India Today* rating, he has gone down slightly. In fact, his decline would have been faster except that expectations from his liberal pronouncements continue to remain high.

Third, the opening of Indian skies has dramatically improved air connectivity. Cut-throat competition in air fares, and commencement of the privatization of the Delhi and Mumbai airports with the promise to replicate this for other airports rightly make Praful Patel a high performer. The agenda of civil aviation reforms is however far from over. A policy has been on the anvil for over a year which will rationalize the burden of sharing on non-commercial routes and a credible regulatory structure for a level playing field awaits legislative approval. Training and skill inculcation, particularly for regulators and traffic controllers in managing congested skies with high safety, remains a challenge.

Fourth, navigating an energy policy which combines long-term energy security with affordability remains elusive. The inability of states to reform their electricity sector stalls progress in reaping the benefits of the Electricity Act, 2003. The endemic problems of the coal sector dent any effort for a coherent energy policy. The flip-flop on petroleum pricing leads to confusion. The current high oil prices are not transient aberrations. While revenues from this sector have traditionally been disproportionate, in the end, its inflationary impact notwithstanding, there is no escape from passing on the burden to consumers. In the long run, this will conserve energy and incentivize investment in alternative energy forms. Murli Deora can improve his overall score in the survey if, coupled with oil diplomacy, practised with great aplomb by his predecessor, he can tackle the politics and economics of oil pricing.

Fifth, the performance of Lalu Prasad Yadav in Railways has been universally rated high. Improving finances while protecting consumers through productivity improvements in wagon loading and turnaround time shows the scope of similar improvements elsewhere. No doubt, in the long run, the wear and tear of tracks, transiting to lighter aluminium-based wagons and improving safety cannot be overlooked. While changing technology paradigms offer infinite scope, productivity-linked improvements may run out of steam and the need for tariff rebalancing, eliminating other subsidies and more aggressive public–private partnership cannot be obviated.

Sixth, the current quota controversy overlooks the more neglected and endemic problem of HRD. It is a pity that the Knowledge Commission is now divided and may be dysfunctional. Improving primary education, filling teacher vacancies, reducing dropout ratios, improving quality particularly in mathematics and science, encouraging greater numbers to seek secondary and higher education and grappling with the challenges of faculty attraction and retention, coupled with autonomy in technical institutes, are areas of far-reaching importance. Regrettably, no road map is in sight. We are frittering away our greatest comparative advantage—a young demographic profile—instead of fostering a knowledge hub.

Seventh, there are other areas where action has scarcely begun, like reforms of the judiciary or labour laws, or where initiatives taken have not yielded outcomes, like an integrated food law. The roads programme has suffered from costly time overruns. Applications for environmental clearance pile up. Maran is a bright spot, but it cannot be said for many other allied partners. It is not surprising that in these areas the concerned ministers have not figured favourably in the survey markings.

Finally, any government must encourage itself by propagating its achievements. The slogan of all-inclusive growth has resulted in tangible initiatives of Bharat Nirman, the Employment Guarantee Scheme, the Urban Renewal Mission, the Sarva Shiksha Abhiyan and the midday meal programme. If implemented with sincerity through a vastly improved public delivery system, particularly in states where governance has been weak, these can make a dramatic difference to rural prosperity. It is however premature to comment on their success.

On the whole, the report presents a mixed picture. But like all report cards, it is also a ready reckoner of achievements, failures and expectations. Will the prime minister hold a mirror to the faltering performers?

28 May 2006

IX

MANAGING THE ECONOMY

The Planning Commission Needs to Reinvent Itself

The National Development Council has approved the approach to the Eleventh Five Year Plan contained in the document, 'Towards Faster and More Inclusive Growth'.

The council has always been an orderly body. I remember no occasion in which it turned down a five-year plan. Chief ministers, being politically savvy, are keen on reciting the achievements of their state, and, with some exceptions, rarely comment on any analytical or ideological weaknesses in the proposal. Besides, keeping the centre happy allows them to seek special favours later.

The document cleared recently is more than a marginal improvement over its predecessors. It is readable, not too lengthy, covers the key issues and undertakes obligations on several targets that can be monitored. Basically, it believes that a 'feasible objective is to accelerate from 8 per cent growth at the end of the Tenth Plan to 10 per cent at the end of the Eleventh Plan, yielding a GDP growth rate of about 9 per cent in the Eleventh Plan.' This will mean a substantial increase in domestic investment from about 27 per cent in the Tenth Plan to 35 per cent in the Eleventh Plan; this increase would be financed through public and private investment.

Success, like prophecy, is sometimes self-fulfilling. The current economic buoyancy has silenced many critics and masks significant weaknesses.

The revised document, while outlining a coherent strategy, still fails to answer many questions. First, the fiscal. A reference to the vulnerability in the first two years of the plan by 'the lack of sufficient feasibility in fiscal management arising from FRBM Acts in the Centre and the State' leaves one guessing what is really being recommended. A pause button, a relaxation, or a rewriting of the targets themselves contained in the Act? This is important because the huge public investment proposed for irrigation, health, education, Bharat Nirman, the extension of the National Rural Employment Scheme to cover all districts, crop insurance and ambitious social security programmes for the unorganized sector will need substantial increase in public investment.

Given the present fiscal targets under the Acts, even the anticipated increase in the Gross Budgetary Support (a name for the resources set apart in the budget to support planned expenditure) may not get accommodated even while this increase itself remains grossly inadequate.

Besides, if fiscal targets are breached by the Centre, the states cannot be kept on a leash to adhere to the targets prescribed for them. You cannot have one set of rules for the Centre, another for the states.

Second, the targeted increase in foreign investment requires fresh thinking and strategy which have not been spelled out. Even on the contentious issue of labour policy, after making out a fairly cogent case for labour reforms, it prefers to say that 'there are different views on the actual impact of these laws on employment'. True, but where does that leave us?

Third, a substantial part of the increase in public investment assumes improved management of non-plan expenditure, particularly, better targeting of subsidies and application of users' charges. We have said these things before, but there is little evidence to suggest any tangible improvement. Some states have chosen to go forward and we hope the others will follow but this may not be adequate. The power sector, particularly, remains problematic. Expectations that states will bring down transmission and distribution losses from the current 40 per cent to at least 15 per cent borders on wishful thinking. In no other area have policy prescriptions gone so awry as in power reforms. Yet, this is the centrepiece of a lot of other measures to keep us competitive and spur investment.

Fourth, a lot of reliance has been placed on public–private partnership. Apart from infrastructure, one area where this is greatly needed is in vocational and higher education.

The plan has rightly recognized that only 10 per cent of the relevant age group go to universities against 25 per cent in most developing countries and there is an overwhelming need to undertake major expansion.

Providing incentives to private investment is inescapable. But how can all this happen without significant reforms in the education sector, where notwithstanding the Knowledge Commission, no coherent road map is evident? Subsisting prejudices and exaggerated fears persist.

In conclusion, the Planning Commission has served us well in putting out a candid document. The expectations on growth trends and other socio-economic targets are dependent on multiple policy measures embedded in the document. Many unresolved issues elude public consensus.

Coalition politics does not help in times like these. Some states are willing to take difficult decisions. However, this is a good time for the centre to end prevarication and begin action.

The Planning Commission may need to reinvent itself. Public investment, for a long time, will continue to play a significant, if not a dominant role in our economy. Surely, as the custodian of our future economic strategy it is much more than a mere think tank. The implementation of the policy content of what has been approved makes the commission accountable in multiple ways.

The Planning Commission, created by government notification, is not a statutory body. Nonetheless, its pejorative description as an extra-constitutional body is unfair. However, it must develop the institutional clout for others to listen and act on the agreed policies. The implementation of the Eleventh Plan will test this ability in full measure.

10 December 2006

50

The Eleventh Plan: Going beyond Platitudes

The parliament has been preoccupied with issues like the leakage of the Pathak report and a privilege motion to consider our multiple economic challenges. Last week I had written about some preconditions necessary for a successful Eleventh Five Year Plan. I realize that not all of these conditions can be met, but there are some on which concerted action can make a difference; like reclassification of accounts and a vastly improved design for centrally sponsored schemes. Here, I propose to deal with some critical choices which need to be made by the Planning Commission before presenting the Approach Paper to the National Development Council.

First, for an 8–9 per cent rate of growth, the domestic rate of savings must increase from around 27.1 per cent to 32.3 per cent. This has been predicated on a marginal increase in household savings but a substantial increase in government savings from a negative figure to a positive 2.6 per cent. Where are the government savings expected to come from, especially as privatization has come to a halt? Increasing the tax ratio has been proposed, but this could adversely impact private savings with an uncertain impact on the overall savings rate. Besides, the assumed elasticity of private savings to net income has not been explained.

Second, there has been considerable controversy surrounding the Fiscal Responsibility and Budget Management (FRBM) Act. What are the assumptions underlying the discussion about the timing of priority expenditures versus enforcement of the FRBM—how could we know that delaying the FRBM targets by X years would be enough time to begin accomplishing these goals? What about implementation difficulties? What would be a credible time for resuming attention on fiscal responsibility targets? What would reassure international investors that the relaxation was temporary? I doubt many would argue that India should *not* invest in infrastructure and social services, but some kind of credible plan for implementation and for a time-bound return to fiscal discipline is essential, especially in the light of investment requirements. The statement about shifting the targets to be 'cyclically adjusted in keeping with international best practices' is a little misleading here, as the implication is that relaxing the FRBM targets for a few years to enable expenditure on infrastructure and social priorities would be consistent with 'best practices'. These 'best practices' cyclically adjusted budget rules, however, typically vary the target according to a transparent formula linked to overall macro indicators.

Third, the Plan is somewhat vague on the macro fundamentals. Some clarification is needed on the feasibility of the targets and assumptions as outlined here:

- Where do the investment rates and domestic savings rates required for different growth targets come from? What kind of macroeconomic model and what kind of assumptions?
- What is the strategy for increasing the private sector's willingness to invest? Some essential investments are mentioned—infrastructure, education, among them—but what about specific ways to increase the private sector's willingness? The discussion on enabling programmes for PPP in the Plan is vague; recommendations that the process 'be seen to provide services at reasonable cost and in a transparent manner' are easier said than done.
- What would be the strategy for addressing an endogenous business cycle? Wouldn't early recognition, with fiscal and monetary response, further affect expectations? Besides, what does endogenous mean? Does it mean politically induced business cycles?
- Fourth, the introduction makes the valuable point that 'the private

> sector, including farming, small scale enterprises and the corporate sector' would need to play an even more important role. But there is no discussion of what might be the comparative advantages of the public vs private sectors, or what might be the complementarities or, most importantly, what might be the most effective way to use public resources to leverage private resources.

As part of this framework, we also need to be realistic in our expectations of what the private sector will and will not do. For example, the private sector can be relied upon to finance some infrastructure, but the political risk premium for projects located in some lawless areas may just be too high for private companies and these might be areas to which public resources would need to be directed. There are other areas where we need to be more explicit in our recommendations, like a clearer enunciation of policies to attract direct foreign investment, for instance merely to say that foreign investors have shown strong interest in playing a larger role in multi-branded retail stores is not enough. Removal of sector caps, particularly in insurance, banking and some others and enabling legislation in key areas like coal and mines remain critical. Engaging states for greater diversification, including market linkage supported by modern marketing process, and abolition of the Agriculture Produce Marketing Act needs proactive action. Similarly, merely to say that to retain competitive advantage we need greater flexibility in labour laws is not enough. Can we at least recommend that the flexibility should be available prospectively or that it would not apply to SPVs or to empower the states to devise policy configurations best suited to their needs? The Planning Commission must be complemented on putting contentious issues in the domain of public discussion. However, at some point discussions must be replaced by decisions. Hopefully, the final documents will make more categorical recommendations than platitudes in carefully balanced formulations. Ambiguity, particularly in coalition politics, may have some advantages but implementation must go beyond such ambiguities.

13 August 2006

The Eleventh Plan, or the Eleventh Version of the Same Plan?

The parliament is preoccupied with the 'mole' hinted in Jaswant Singh's book and in the midst of all this has also passed the Office of Profit Bill. Since the future of several important financial legislations remains in doubt, the only economic issue which has received parliamentary attention is the price rise and farmers' woes. These deserve all the attention they can get. However, before parliament meets for its winter session, the Approach to the Eleventh Five Year Plan would have been endorsed by the National Development Council. The parliament is a recipient but has never been a forum for discussing five year plans or our medium-term economic strategy, which the plans are designed to articulate. While it is true that five year plans do not technically require parliamentary approval and no legislation is involved, they increasingly signal our policy directions.

Sectoral issues are sometimes discussed in the standing committee. The general debate following the presentation of the budget focuses primarily on the annual budgetary appropriations. These are not a substitute for a more searching discussion on key economic issues, choices and options. The state of the economy receives scant attention.

So let me, in this essay, pose some issues which deserve broader attention. First, let me consider the pre-conditions followed by a consideration of policy options. The approach paper, called 'Towards Faster and More Inclusive Growth', makes many statements about the role of the states and the centre, leading to an overall impression that the states will be asked to take more ownership and be more accountable for their programmes while at the same time 'backward' areas will be brought into inclusive growth. This is an important direction, and we have to think about the structure of fiscal incentives to create this kind of shift. On the whole, a rethink of the transfer system is needed to reconcile the goals of having performance-linked transfers and inclusive growth, the two priorities mentioned in the plan. On the one hand, performance-linked transfers reward good performance and good performers. On the other hand, inclusive growth needs to ensure that the bad performers are not permanently left behind. How do we motivate the lagging states without giving up on them? This is a complex task, with many interested parties and there are incremental steps that could be taken at least to create more transparency in the fiscal transfers.

Second, on rates of growth, the Eleventh Plan expects an overall growth of 8.5 per cent of GDP which implies even higher growth in the terminal years, necessitating the investment-gearing ratio to increase from 31 per cent to 38 per cent. This entails an increase in the domestic savings rate as well as access to external resources including a sharp increase in direct foreign investment. Alternative options and growth targets need to be spelt out both in terms of their consequences on poverty reduction and employment generation.

Third, the disability which faces five year plans is that given the present electoral cycle, it commences at the mid-point of the government in office. Given anti-incumbency factors with every change of government, a mid-term appraisal which basically outlines altered priorities and strategies creates discontinuities. Hardly have departments begun serious implementation of the plan that electoral discontinuities and revised mandates lead to new approaches and strategies. Electoral cycles can neither be retarded nor advanced to synchronize with five year plans and yet these plans are designed as politico-economic statements of the government in office. Besides, if governments do not complete their full term, fine-tuning these five year plan cycles cannot be easy.

One alternative, of course an extreme one, is not to have five year plans at all but to articulate a medium-term strategy and move to a regime of rolling plans in which priorities and strategies are easier to alter. Besides, project implementation is an ongoing process and annual budgetary appropriations can be predicted but not assumed.

Fourth, the synchronization of five year plans with the recommendations of the Finance Commission is another contentious issue. States find it difficult to foresee the quantum of resources which would be available given multiple sources of resource flows where the Planning Commission's recommendations are made one year, the Finance Commission's another year and the centrally sponsored schemes have their own time frame for resource flows. The Planning Commission and Finance Commission disconnect is specially worrisome because the total resources available to the states under the plan depends on the states' own contribution, which comes partly from the Finance Commission and another part from their resources. Since synchronization of electoral cycles with five year plans is more complex, the least we can do is to synchronize the plan with the cycle of the Finance Commission. The Finance Commission is constitutionally mandated and its recommendations viewed as awards and there may be multiple advantages in linking the plans and commencing them immediately after recommendations of the Finance Commission. This would enable states to plan on the basis of more predictable resource flows.

Fifth, another issue raised by the Planning Commission is the irrational distinction between revenue and capital expenditure. It has brought out clearly that such a distinction (particularly the target to eliminate revenue deficit completely by 2008) is flawed since expenditures in the critical social sector which have a multiplier effect on development are classified as revenue expenditure and indeed, far from being eliminated, should be strengthened. While this dichotomy between revenue and capital expenditure is certainly flawed, so is the distinction in many areas between plan and non-plan. Several items booked under the non-plan expenditure have beneficial development consequences in improving overall investment environment. Reclassification of government accounts must be a critical starting point and this would require coordinated efforts by the Comptroller and Auditor General, Controller of Civil Accounts,

Ministry of Finance as well as the Planning Commission. The exercise to bring greater sanity in such classification will not be easy. There may be merit in government appointing a high-level Accounts Reclassification Committee with a former CAG, Expenditure Secretary and Planning Commission to make recommendations which can be reflected in the Eleventh Plan itself. We must learn from the past. Devoting attention to these preconditions will lay the foundations of successful five year plans. Nobody wants the plan to be the eleventh version of the same plan.

6 August 2006

52

Put the Finance Ministry on the Reforms Path

The parliament is in recess. While the press survives the silly season, ministers get respite to plan for the future. Chidambaram has already initiated a pre-budget exercise to rewrite the Income Tax Act. This is also a good time for him to reflect on what else he can do which does not get mired in controversy. His second term as finance minister has modest success to his credit; bold ideas and initiatives have been stalled in the quagmire of coalition politics. He has as many detractors within the government as among the allies. Given these limitations, there are some areas which are non-contentious and can result in public good.

- First and foremost, to complete the agenda of tax reforms. The exercise to rewrite a new Income Tax Act was initiated by him in 1997 but implementation of the Easwaran Committee Report was overtaken by events. Since then, there have been a number of changes in the tax law. A new act which is written simply, using non-technical language which can be understood by the average man would be widely appreciated. One bad example was the self-filing Income Tax Return programme called Saral (simple) but which, in effect, was *jatil* (complicated). That is a route which must be avoided. We must also enlarge the scope for self-filing and self-assessment of tax returns; the forms can be retained by the assesses themselves while paying off their liability. When in doubt, the returns can be sought by the assessing officer. Otherwise, gathering returns whose custody is onerous merely adds to work, congests space and creates an adversarial culture.

- Second, any reorganization of the revenue department should include better coordination among its multiple intelligence agencies. The Central Board of Direct Taxes (CBDT) has an investigation division with field formations for gathering intelligence on tax evasion. It also conducts searches and carries out investigations in cases of tax evasion. I guess while this is necessary both as a deterrent and for enforcing compliance, revamping the present system by increasingly replacing overt action through investigative audit needs consideration. At any rate, the obnoxious practice7—sometimes followed in the past—of giving field officers targets on numbers of cases, raids and seizures needs to end.

  The Central Board of Excise and Customs (CBEC) has a Directorate General of Revenue Intelligence (DGRI), a Directorate General of Anti-Evasion and a Directorate of Preventive Operations. In addition, there is the Central Economic Intelligence Bureau (CEIB) and the Directorate of Enforcement. The Directorate of Enforcement, with the repeal of the Foreign Exchange Regulation Act (FERA), is concerned with the adjudication of earlier cases. The high pendency of earlier cases which have gone on endlessly is a source of interminable harassment. The Enforcement Directorate also implements the FEMA and the Prevention of Money Laundering Act. The CEIB, which has an Economic Intelligence Council, coordinates the intelligence functions of the Intelligence Bureau, RAW, and the Narcotics Control Bureau and has functions which are similar to the Directorate General of Revenue Intelligence. Clearly, both the DGRI and the CEIB need to be merged. DGRI is an older organization with considerable expertise and can effectively absorb the functions of the CEIB. In addition to this, the functions of the Directorate General of Anti-Evasion and the Directorate of Preventive Operations can also be merged.
- Third, the present acts being administered by the revenue

department need major simplification. In the area of direct taxes, all existing acts which are still relevant should be merged with the Income Tax Act and the Wealth Tax Act.

In the area of indirect taxes major changes are needed. The acts include the Conservation of Foreign Exchange and Prevention of Smuggling Activities Act, 1974 (COFEPOSA), whose main purpose is 'to provide for preventive detention in certain cases for the purposes of conservation and augmentation of foreign exchange and prevention of smuggling activities and for matters connected therewith'. This is a draconian act, because apart from detention powers, its definition is wide to include anyone engaging in smuggling, keeping smuggled goods, engaging in transport of smuggled goods, harbouring such persons and particularly specifies areas which are highly vulnerable to smuggling, etc.

To buttress this act, there is another legislation, the Smugglers and Foreign Exchange Manipulators (Forfeiture of Property) Act, 1976, (SAFEMA) designed 'for the forfeiture of illegally acquired properties of smugglers and foreign exchange manipulators since smuggling of foreign exchange manipulation have a deleterious effect on the national economy.' As if this were not enough, there is an Appellate Tribunal for Forfeited Property (ATFP) which hears appeals against orders passed under the SAFEMA. We have an entire hierarchy of organizations dealing with the conservation of foreign exchange with preventive detention, investigation, enforcement, forfeiture of properties and appeals.

At a time when FERA, the primary act for enforcing foreign exchange rule violation, has been replaced by FEMA, making it a civil compoundable offence, to keep a preventive detention act, COFEPOSA, and the forfeiture of property act, SAFEMA, is untenable. Offences connected with smuggling are adequately covered by the Customs Act, 1962, which, if need be, can be strengthened. India takes pride in the abundance of its foreign exchange. The Reserve Bank of India, notwithstanding neutral postures, intervenes discreetly to prevent excessive appreciation of the rupee. It is ironic that while one arm, namely the Economic Affairs Wing and the RBI, proposes clever financial engineering to prevent excessive reserve accumulation, the other arm, the revenue department, is busy detaining people for preventing the augmentation of foreign exchange. We have the problem of plenty instead of scarcity; continuing the COFEPOSA and the SAFEMA is incongruous with contemporary reality. They have increasingly become a source of harassment, manipulation and corruption.

- Fourth, the expenditure department faces two challenges:
  i. Devising a credible expenditure tracking and evaluation system in line with the presentation of Chidambaram's recent outlay–outcome document to parliament and which can truly enforce performance budgeting.
  ii. Resolving the dichotomy in the accountability of financial advisers—torn as they are between the allegiance to their administrative ministry which prefer somewhat lax expenditure control and the MoF seeking rigorous enforcement of expenditure norms.
- Fifth, the department of economic affairs needs a rejig. Bilateral assistance and even multilateral aid flows have ceased to be our dominant concerns. Nor should the ministry, say, be looking after currency, coinage and government mints which should be transferred to the RBI. Reorganizing divisions to focus on infrastructure, investment and play a catalytic role for coordinating economic reforms in other ministries should be the dominant concerns.

Reforming the finance ministry to meet contemporary challenges deserves serious attention. Earlier committee reports were either ad hoc, impractical or flawed. Chidambaram can use the period between now and the next session of parliament to initiate serious action. This could signal other ministries to undertake similar efforts. A reformed finance ministry is central in implementing the multiple promises and challenges of the UPA government. The compulsion to readapt economic policies to meet the needs of altered times makes this inescapable.

11 September 2005

53

Bridging the Gap between Outlays and Outcomes

Last week, P. Chidambaram presented to the parliament the 'Outlays and Outcomes Budget—Towards Achieving Better Results'. He described it as 'historic', fulfilling a budget commitment made at the instance of the prime minister. At a time when public outlays increase rapidly, there is understandable concern on how well the money is spent and whether the desired objectives are met. For instance, an average man is not particularly enamoured about enhanced outlays for power or education unless this translates into easier and more affordable power or better schools in his neighbourhood.

Outlays are generally perceived as meaningless statistics. This 700-page mammoth document now compiles expenditure outlays, the physical targets, deliverable outcomes and their time frame for implementation. Actually these data were available all the time, because that is how the expenditure outlays are normally approved. Their presentation in a single document to parliament enhances accountability and the obligation to implement them. Coupled with the citizens charter and the Right to Information Act, it empowers beneficiaries to agitate for improved delivery systems.

Nonetheless, this initial exercise only leaves many issues unresolved:

First and foremost, the issue of intuitional coherence. The ministry of statistics and programme implementation came into effect on 9

April 1999 by merging the departments of statistics and programme implementation. They were more or less expected to do what Chidambaram has now presented to parliament. Their twenty-point programme division (in operation since 1 April 1986) was to 'monitor schemes relating to poverty alleviation, employment generation, health and education and report on quality of life specially those below the poverty line'. The infrastructure division was 'to monitor infrastructure projects in Coal, Power, Steel, Railways, Telecom, Civil Aviation and Roads and to compile monthly data on the progress'. The project monitoring division was 'to monitor all central outlays above 20 crores and to examine time and cost overruns as well as identify bottlenecks'. Unfortunately, the department became a dumping ground for unwanted officials. Its monthly reports are badly brought out, fail to read coherently and rarely served any useful purpose for policy makers to consider changes in the approach to project implementation. Their 'Flash Reports' were meaningless statistics; no one was moved, much less motivated to act.

Recently, a new entity called the 'Programme Outcome and Response Monitoring Division' (PO&RM) has been created in the Planning Commission to inter alia 'identify deficiencies, to collect, collate and analyse relevant data for outcome monitoring'. This division, headed by Nandini Azad, brings in rich NGO experience and has got off to a credible start, earning the appreciation of the prime minister. The programme implementation department should be merged with this division and assigned an independent status to ensure neutrality, reporting their findings to the prime minister.

Data collection from multiple agencies including government, both central and the states, their statistical offices, target beneficiaries and civil society must be politically neutral, credible and efficacious in cost. Developing non-adversarial lines of communication with multiple agencies needs imagination and trust.

Second, developing a methodology of programme evaluation is complex. Earlier efforts at 'performance budgeting' where annual outlays are conditional on earlier performance remained unsuccessful. 'Causal effects' of 'conditions before' and 'after the programme' are often not easy to establish. International initiatives like the World Bank's statistical capacity-building projects and the formation of inter-agency organizations like PARIS21 have multiple lessons for us.

Third, monitoring outcomes raise conceptually difficult issues. The correlation between outlay and physical activity is more straightforward and Chidambaram's outcome budget document can be a guide. However, auditing outcomes by a central organization can be either through what is called the 'police patrol' method in the literature on bureaucracy or via a public oversight called the 'fire alarm'.

Police patrol means that the auditor keeps an eye on things that go wrong and verify money has been spent, while the fire alarm requires certification on implementation to meet beneficiaries' expectations. Beneficiaries can raise an alarm if the programme has either failed or has failed to benefit them. Is the Nandini Azad monitoring unit going to be a police patrol or a fire alarm? The department of expenditure remains responsible for performance budgeting and, what is crucial, approving budget outlays. The role of the Comptroller and Auditor General which is confined to ex post expenditure audit and evaluation also needs to be meshed in any new institutional structure.

Fourth, the issue of how effective is the programme is a much harder question. It is hard to draw inferences about whether something worked by comparison of what happened before it and what happened after. Drawing conclusions about food subsidies that reduced malnutrition or parent oversight boards that improved village schools through higher attendance, ensured better teacher attendance and whether a programme made any decisive difference remain problematic. The process of 'before-and-after comparison' should ensure that the selection of the group for evaluation is truly random, 'a cross-section over a rolling schedule' and is not designed to ensure any desired evaluation outcome.

Besides, the question of how to assess the true value of goods and services and the true cost of inputs raises the issue of shadow pricing. Arnold Harberger raises methodological issues like the reflection of capital market distortions, use of so-called 'border prices' or 'national prices' in putting a value on projects' benefits and cost and how distributional weights can be used in valuing benefits and costs by different groups. Similarly, Aristides Torche describes various forms adopted for project evaluation methodology for assessing social programme benefits. The methodology used by the UNDP in their 'Handbook for Monitoring and Evaluating' results has some useful suggestions on developing baseline data for making comparisons over time and the activity schedule of the project.

Finally, determining sustainability and long-term impact is crucial for project outcomes. The post-project era must result in sustainable poverty reduction, life quality improvement and the multiplier effects through diversified economic activity resulting in durable benefits.

The current focus on programme outcomes is a starting point. It is a first step in seeking symmetry between outlays, financial expenditure and physical activity. Assigning accountability for outcomes has proved elusive. Prehistoric approaches cannot result in historic outcomes! Evaluation outlays must resolve issues of institutional coherence, credibility of data collection and evolving acceptable methodologies to evaluate project outcomes and their long-term impact on intended beneficiaries. It will be a learning curve. Bridging the chasm between outcome and outlay is a daunting challenge. Chidambaram has made a credible beginning.

4 September 2005

54

Foreign Exchange Reserves Are No Magic Wand

The proposal for a more productive use of our foreign exchange reserves has received mixed response which is not surprising. Both sides are reasonably familiar with each other's arguments. It is said that what we profess is what we are expected to profess. Historically, the Planning Commission has believed that the finance ministry is short-sighted, niggardly, preoccupied with a fiscal fetish while what is important is high growth, which, in the long run, will also generate larger revenue streams. As long as public expenditure is targeted to capital-creating assets like strengthening infrastructure and we can build on the virtuous circles which growth creates, a temporary fiscal deterioration is acceptable. The finance ministry, on the other hand, believes that productivity of expenditure is difficult to measure, much less monitor, there is irreversibility on expenditure commitments once made, and fiscal deterioration, apart from crowding out private investments, makes micromanagement more difficult. It also sends negative signals to multilateral institutions, credit-rating agencies and potential foreign investors. The truth perhaps lies somewhere in between.

It is ironic that successive deputy chairmen of the Planning Commission speak one language when they are in the Yojana Bhawan and another on becoming finance ministers. The interchangeability has happened more than once involving distinguished personalities like N.D. Tiwari, Pranab Mukherjee and Jaswant Singh to name a few. The 'halo' any deputy chairman acquires in the Yojana Bhawan is related to his success in garnering as much resources as possible (popularly known as gross budgetary support—GBS) and in getting prime ministers to overrule the niggardly finance ministry! The present deputy chairman, who knows both sides of the story, has done well in suggesting some clever financial engineering to increase the resource kitty of the Planning Commission and at the same time, persuade Chidambaram that this won't hurt his fiscal numbers as presented to parliament. So what can be better if growth is fostered and fiscal deficit as a consequence does not deteriorate.

The proposal is to utilize US $5 billion per annum of reserves for the next two years to finance high import-intensive infrastructure projects with suitable calibration in import duty. The government would be increasing its deficit through issuing securities, with the RBI monetizing part of this deficit by picking up these securities and the rupee resources obtained by the government being used to purchase foreign exchange of the equivalent amount and utilize them towards financing preferably 100 per cent imported infrastructure projects.

The key question which arises is the following: Is there need for greater public investment in infrastructure? It would be difficult to argue against the merits of doing so. The cost and quality of power remain exceptionally high; port constraints make trade expensive; airports need enlargements; telecom requires rural connectivity; the national highways and the rural network need huge resources for timely completion; while the railways need investments for safety, modernization and faster trains on commercially viable corridors.

The following issue would however needs to be addressed: Is poor infrastructure a result of inadequate resources? We all know that each year finance ministers are able to show somewhat improved fiscal performance emanating from the underutilization of funds either from tardy defence purchases or inadequate plan expenditure. Even during the current year, there is a utilization slack in ports, power and other infrastructure areas. So the ability of the public sectors to efficiently spend resources poses endemic challenges in improving the quality of public services which have deteriorated in recent times.

The issue of public expenditure versus private expenditure or what has become fashionable public–private partnership needs to be addressed. If deregulation creates new space for private investment, the sectors or segments which need continued public funding need delineation. Assuming that private investment is still shy while infrastructure improvement can brook no delay, the issue of inadequate sector reforms looms large. Private investment in power remains shy because power sector reforms notwithstanding, the Electricity Bill, 2003, still needs credible implementation, particularly by many state governments. Building new electricity projects by financially sick electricity boards or NTPC taking up more national projects without sector reforms is not sustainable. Similarly, strengthening the railways' Golden Quadrilateral and modernizing and upgrading tracks are inescapable but cannot be a substitute for long-overdue railway reforms. These inter alia include a sunset clause for distortionary rail tariff between passenger and freight, depoliticization of railway tariff fixation, corporatization of several activities on which experts agree. Montek has been a strong votary against entitlement-driven devolution with a preference for performance-based access. This principle can hardly be given a go-by in the present debate. Since the foreign exchange reserve is essentially not government money against which it is proposed to issue bonds, there are still several choices open to us. The first option is to temporarily extend the date by which the agreement with the RBI on the borrowing limit by the government becomes fully operational. The full prohibition from subscribing to the government's securities in the primary issue stage only clicks in 2007. This can yield low-cost finance for infrastructure projects. A temporary extension of this agreement may be preferable than an amendment of the Fiscal Responsibility Management Act itself whose enactment was not easy to achieve. The second option is along the lines of the Planning Commission's proposal by utilizing the foreign exchange reserves and issue of securities with monetization of the fiscal deficit. The third option is to recognize that the additionality of expenditure on infrastructure has a compelling economic and social case and accept an additional fiscal deficit of 0.5 per cent to 0.75 per cent per annum in larger interest. The fourth is to concentrate for a year or two on the quality of public expenditure, complete ongoing sector reforms, rationalize public portfolios and reprioritize expenditure. In the public debate, these options and their implications need closer examination. The issue is as much about the modality of financing as about the quality of public expenditure, effectiveness of delivery system and the underpinning of sector reforms. At the same time, while in the present climate it may be fashionable to find clever ways to enhance public expenditure, this is no substitute for addressing the more endemic sector problems. Montek has the credit for raising a public debate on these issues since urgent infrastructure improvement has overwhelming multiplier benefit. The prime minister's call for an early consensus on these options has struck the right chord. Foreign exchange plenty by itself is no magic wand for our economic ills.

21 November 2004

X

STATES OF THE UNION

55

Ask the Right Questions for the Correct Diagnosis

It is not the policies that are failing so much as the machinery for implementing them.

This was the *Economist*'s assessment in an article appearing on 1 June 2006 of the reasons for India's persistent failure to provide quality infrastructure and social services. It is easy to support this assessment with outcome statistics, summaries of slippage from promises and targets, cost overruns and even simply, public opinion polls. It is harder to see how to reverse this 'failure of the machinery'.

There are several challenges. First, asking the questions that help distinguish between appropriate responses. Second, prioritizing the search for answers to minimize costs. Finally, detailed information on performance has to be widely available and accessibly summarized to maintain the incentives to acknowledge and address failure.

Take, for example, the widespread and long-standing failure to spend allocated funds. Once a year or so, the media pillories the central and the state governments for not spending their allocations for rural roads, electrification, or other programmes. The finance ministry and the Planning Commission spar about whether the 'surrenders' should lead to reduced allocations next year. And then the next round of allocations comes.

The generic solutions have been unsuccessful. 'Performance management' can mean many things. Zero-based budgeting that reduces budgets proportionally to the surrenders could only encourage departments to get better at wasting funds, unless the monitoring of impact and project quality improves. Cutting programmes that have surrendered funds runs the risk of punishing people for a state's failures.

Asking a few questions to determine where the machinery is breaking down would be a more specific solution. This is simple as we are not questioning the allocation of funds, or trying to evaluate the impact of the programme, but just identifying the weak links in the disbursement process as we head into a budget season in which more funds will be allocated.

First, does the machinery fail at the project proposal level? Are there no projects in the pipeline, either approved or pending approval? Is there a high rejection rate for projects being evaluated for funding? It is entirely plausible that there are not enough quality projects. The state cadres are understaffed, and positions for engineers, surveyors and other skilled employees tend to have a higher vacancy rate.

If this is the case, one solution would be to open the proposal process to allow the social sector to prepare project proposals, along the lines of the demand-driven social investment funds used around the world.

Another solution would be to depute trained personnel from the central government to aid with project preparation and training project preparation skills.

If there are quality projects in the pipeline, however, this approach would be a waste of resources. The next question would be whether project approvals are the problem. Is there a backlog of proposals, with limited numbers approved? Is it a failure at the state or central government project evaluation levels? This, again, is entirely plausible, but suggests something other than a failure in project proposals.

Resources would have to be directed at training evaluators and streamlining the evaluation process instead of encouraging more projects. Standardizing and computerizing project proposals would speed up evaluation but the expense would be less justifiable if the main constraint on spending were in fact a lack of proposals.

It is also possible that allocated funds are not spent because the states do not provide adequate counterpart funds. The absence of counterpart funds, in and of itself, is not terribly informative—all it means is that the state government's costs of obtaining the funds (in terms of bureaucratic hurdles or loss of programme control) are greater than the benefits of having the additional resources. Is this because the costs are 'too high'? What are the most costly hurdles? Or is it because the benefits of the programme are 'too low'? And if the benefits are too low, would people rather spend limited funds on something else, or is the state government not accountable to its citizens?

One option is to subject the 'benefits' side to public scrutiny. Support accountability by publicizing the list of all relevant projects where money was allocated but not disbursed because the state failed to provide counterpart funding. If states are still not providing counterpart funding after several years with this kind of scrutiny possible, it would be safer to assume that the state population has other ideas about how to use the funds.

The cost side could be disentangled with a survey of the users—state governments—that identified the most common complaints. Business and research organizations carry out business climate surveys asking firms to identify constraints. Why not have a public sector analogue asking state officials to identify constraints? This would be an essential step towards making the general recommendation to 'streamline' more specifically focused on high-return adjustments. However, the costs of preparing this survey might not be the highest priority for funding if the surrenders were due to a lack of project proposals or bottlenecks in evaluation.

It is possible that answers to these questions are available. This would only make it worse that the problems remain unaddressed. It is central to finalizing all relevant annual expenditure budgets. We need the vision to repair.

With Jessica Wallack
14 January 2007

56

Centre and the States—a New Compact

Last week (in the beginning of August 2005), I wrote about the central government focusing on their achievements and inadequacies. This week I want to focus on the states. It is now almost a cliché that action lies with the states. An 8 per cent growth requires much greater engagement of states—be it in power, roads, VAT, education, health, agriculture and rural development, to name a few. We have long talked about these issues, some individual chief ministers have excelled but concerted action is missing. It is to the credit of *India Today* that they recognized this some time ago and for the third successive year hosted the 'India Today Conclave of Chief Ministers' on 5 August 2005. As a backdrop to these discussions, rigorous work undertaken by Bibek Debroy and Leevesh Bhandari assessed, evaluated and ranked the states based on key growth parameters. Notwithstanding disappointment or protests from the losers or exuberance from the winners, the event creates an atmosphere that encourages one to strive for betterment.

Losers are nudged to improve, winners are challenged to sustain. In 2005, fifteen chief ministers attended, but the absence of representatives of southern states was somewhat disappointing. Discussion centred on seven issues, namely, matching outlays with outcomes, the need for smaller states, the choice between free or fair power to farmers, implementation of VAT, the future of privatization and the intertwining of good economics with good politics. All this is at the core of our growth strategy. Aroon Purie got the conference to a good start. Both Prabhu Chawla and Jairam Ramesh moderated well, Prabhu in his inimitable *Seedhi Baat* style, while Jairam was provocative but non-partisan.

Many issues eluded consensus. Smaller states may have the advantages of better supervision but were contentious, lacking in scale externalities with reduced political clout. On power, most of the states were not in favour of free power although Amarinder Singh, with impending elections, argued that the inadequacy of the Minimum Support Price which does not reflect rising costs entitles farmers to this extra compensation.

Narendra Modi's suggestion was cleverly diversionary on his priority on water instead of power. On VAT, given the political divide, a new White Paper on VAT based on the recent experience with a firmer time table for phasing out of CST was favoured.

Non-conforming states need a face-saving formula. There was consensus on one issue. Vasundhara Raje credibly argued the case for an improved institutional mechanism for Centre–state dialogue explaining that the Sarkaria Commission Report was submitted in the 1980s and that the new economic challenges need fresh thinking. In fact, the national Common Minimum Programme has suggested the creation of a new commission on Centre—state relations. When constituted, it will be a while before they recommend measures and even longer before those measures are implemented. What are the existing institutions for this dialogue? First and foremost, the National Development Council (NDC) was constituted in August 1952 following the formation of the Planning Commission on 15 March 1950. Initially, its functions were 'to strengthen and mobilize the efforts of the nation in support of Five Year Plans and to promote economic policies and to ensure a balanced and rapid development in all parts of the country'.

Much later, following the recommendations of the Administrative Reforms Commission, 1967, the functions of the NDC were enlarged to 'include preparation of guidelines for the formulation of national plan, including assessment of resources, and to consider the important questions of social and economic policies affecting national development'. Second are the Zonal Councils mooted by Jawaharlal Nehru in 1956 during the course of the submission of the Report of the States Reorganization Commission suggesting that states be grouped into four or five zones 'and the Council could develop the habit of co-operative working among the states' acting as a forerunner of the need for regional cooperation with shared commonalities of endowments. The third is the Interstate Council formed on 28 May 1990 based on the recommendations of the Sarkaria Commission. This has been set up under Article 263 of the Constitution which lays down its functions 'of inquiring and advising on disputes which may have arisen between states, discussing subjects in which some or all the states or the Union have common interest and to make recommendations for better co-ordination on such subjects'.

It is surprising that although as early as in the 1950s the Second Finance Commission had recommended the constitution of this Council, it had to await the Sarkaria Commission Report in 1987 to be constituted a few years later. Clearly, times were different. A more homogeneous government at the centre and the states, settled paradigms on development, the absence of major irritants did not necessitate acting on this enabling provision of the constitution for forty-three years.

Last but not the least is the Finance Commission which every five years deals with devolution to states. Of late, it has also suggested to the states a wider gamut of changes on economic policies. However, this is not a continuing body for interactive dialogue.

Over time, regrettably, the NDC has degenerated into a mechanical affair where bored chief ministers listen to long, written speeches of their colleagues with no interaction between themselves and at the end triumphantly adopt either a five year plan or its mid-term review. The structure of the meeting hardly fosters any worthwhile dialogue among the participants. Chief ministers troop out to get photographed, which are published prominently in regional newspapers, suggesting huge achievements by the state! Everybody goes back to sleep till the next meeting is held. Clearly, the NDC is hardly fulfilling its mandate 'of considering issues of economic and social policies affecting national development'.

The Zonal Councils have also lost focus. Interstate Councils meet with periodicity depending on the initiative of the home minister with a flurry of activity on pending regional projects prior to a meeting with tardy follow-up action. India has outgrown either these institutions or at least the way in which they are run. If the India Today Conclave generates so much interaction, why not these bodies of long standing? Economic policy making in key areas needs the concert of states.

14 August 2005

57

Revisiting the Centre–State Divide

The recent India Today Conclave focused on the theme, 'India tomorrow: Bridging the divide'. Over the years, this annual event has forged constructive dialogue on our contemporary challenges. Aroon Purie rightly described these as evolving a commonality of approach 'from the clash of ideas'. This year brought together academia and policy makers to deliberate on multiple facets of divisiveness—global, gender, government versus civil society, immigration, infrastructure and of course, Centre–state relations. Gerhard Schroeder, former chancellor of Germany, was strongly in favour of a multilateral approach on the global challenges of terrorism, energy security, climate change, religious intolerance or the follow-up on trade negotiations. The panels threw up new ideas and innovative approaches on these complex issues. The session, 'Politics: The Centre-State Divide', had Vasundhara Raje and Nitish Kumar as the two panelists. Vasundhara Raje made a forceful presentation on Rajasthan's achievements and plans for higher education, tourism and power. Nitish Kumar outlined his vision for Bihar; while his first priority was improving overall confidence and security, the neglected developmental agenda would get a push. He seemed resolute and sincere.

The state of centre–state relations, however, raises at least three distinct issues. While our federal model has served us well, changing development compulsions, the heterogeneity of governance, the rise of regional parties and the growing income divides need new approaches. First and foremost is the structure of financial devolution.

While the constitutionally mandated Finance Commissions have lent stability while giving emphasis to equity and efficiency, the same cannot be said of other devolutions. The additional central plan flows, though largely formulaic, are not statutorily defined and consultations between states and the Planning Commission are not devoid of quasi-political considerations.

Devolutions through the ministries in respect of central schemes are even less transparent. There is no way to check the allocation of funds across states to evaluate the same for capital and current expenditure or the conditions under which allocations are made. Experts' studies like Indira Rajaraman's 'Is the Indian fiscal federation under threat?' raise serious concerns. Stuti Khemani, in her paper 'Partisan politics and inter-governmental transfers in India', argues, 'a recent surge of empirical studies shows that variations in inter-governmental transfers to sub-national jurisdictions within countries can't be explained by traditional concerns of equity and efficiency alone and political variables representing electoral incentives of public agents are additional and significant determinants.' Looking at the somewhat opaque manner in which ministries allocate funds, it is difficult to collate all funds a state received in a fiscal year and relate these to principles based on either equity or efficiency. The access to externally aided funds is also a complication and despite differences in absorptive capacity or efficiency of utilization, political preference or directional encouragement to lending agencies adds to the distortion. Looking at the transfer system, several improvements seem possible—not only governance and fairness but also efficiency in integrating the myriad forms of transfers that exist today. Higher transparency and coordination would protect these funds from the vagaries of politics and improve utilization.

Second is the absence of a well-functioning institutional mechanism for centre–state dialogue. The National Development Council (NDC) was designed to facilitate such a dialogue but has become a ceremonial body, meeting occasionally to approve five-year plans, mid-term reviews or special reports. The Interstate Council, which was to play a central role in dispute resolution, has not served this purpose either. Except for interstate river disputes independently provided for under the constitution, the Interstate Council has not been active in other areas, which can make it a 'Permanent Adjudication Body'. States continue to complain that unilateral decisions by the central government, as on fiscal issues (like cess, whose realizations are not shared) or compelling states to bear one-fourth of the variable cost under the National Rural Employment Guarantee Act or setting up a new Pay Commission when they have barely emerged from the impact of the Fifth Pay Commission, underscore the need for an active consultative mechanism. The NDC needs redefinition of its mandate and the Interstate Council must be rehoused as part of the prime minister's office, (the prime minister is chairman of the Council) for making the dialogue with the states an ongoing process. This is particularly so when both coalition politics and regional parties are here to stay in the foreseeable future.

Third, given the pace of change, how are recalcitrant states dealt with on issues which are in the domain of states but have national implications? If education or health systems in a state continue to suffer, with thousands of posts of teachers and doctors remaining unfilled, what recourse does the central government have? This embeds a larger policy concern in attempting to balance devolutions to states which are driven by performance criteria through formula-based entitlements. They also need to harmonize considerations of equity with efficiency when the two move in opposite directions. The centre–state divide needs a revisit. Both procedures and institutions need restructuring to meet the new developmental challenges. Everyone knows there is a lack of adequate reforms in power, education, health and agriculture which lie in the purview of the states. We do not have the luxury of time; archaic approaches and institutions are inconsistent with ambitious growth targets. Some things are obvious. These need not await the recommendations of the yet to be constituted commission on centre–state relations. A wake-up call is overdue. These are the three distinct centre–state issues:

- Financial devolution;
- Absence of a well-functioning mechanism for centre–state dialogue; and

- Dealing with recalcitrant status on national issues in the states' domain.

18 March 2006

Building Brand Bihar, the Nalanda Way

Hu Jintao's visit emphasizes the many positives between India and China. Strengthening Indo-Chinese cultural relations can recreate the vision of the educational and cultural affinity that existed between the fourth and the fifteenth centuries. This was epitomized by the Nalanda University. The proposed inauguration of the Hsuan Tsang Memorial Hall in Nalanda in December 2006 reflects the renewed process of cultural revival. Seeking regional consensus to create the new Nalanda University as a centre of educational and cultural excellence, close to the site of the old Nalanda University, has gathered momentum. President Abdul Kalam in his address to the joint session of Bihar legislators articulated this idea and thereafter there have been exchanges with the governments of Singapore, Japan and China. A delegation led by the senior minister of state for foreign affairs of the Singapore government, Balaji Sadasivan visited Bihar in September 2006.

The foreign minister of Singapore, George Yeo, has taken keen personal interest, leading to a recent international seminar with the topic 'Nalanda: Buddhist Cultural Links between Eastern and Southern Asia'. This was jointly promoted by the East Asia Institute, the Institute of South-East Asian Studies, the Institute of South Asian Studies and the Faculty of Arts and Sciences of the National University of Singapore, with the support of the ministry of foreign affairs and the Singapore Buddhist Federation.

It brought together diverse scholars from Japan, China, Sri Lanka,

Vietnam, Malaysia, Cambodia and Thailand apart from India. President Kalam in his keynote address via a live video telecast emphasized that drawing inspiration from the cultural traditions of Nalanda, Bodh Gaya and other Buddhist sites could create a new framework in the modern context to generate and disseminate knowledge and skills to bring about an enlightenment among citizens not just in India but in the region.

Re-establishing Nalanda University would serve as an important cultural link between Southern and East Asia. Foreign Minister George Yeo emphasized the multidimensional influence which Nalanda, as a centre of excellence, could create as an influence centre based on universalism as part of an Asian Renaissance. He said that just as Europe had discovered its cultural roots it was now appropriate for Asia to do so, particularly at a time when the world perceives a shift in the fulcrum of economic power to Asian countries.

I also participated in the seminar and explained that the Nalanda discussions must be perceived in a wider context. The Nalanda University plan itself is part of a larger vision to develop the infrastructure of Bodh Gaya, Gaya, Nalanda and Rajgir as a region to attract the pilgrim, the tourist, and those seeking rejuvenation at the sulphur springs in Rajgir and also to revive the lost educational influence of Nalanda.

The Bihar government has pursued this with zest: land is being acquired and resources have been set aside. Persons of international eminence will be chosen as the chancellor and the vice chancellor. Hopefully, the East Asia Summit in the Philippines and the prime minister's visit to Japan will give the dialogue further momentum. UNESCO and the World Tourism Organization have offered support.

Buddhism needs to be understood in the contemporary context. It has taken multiple forms in Asia. Among the questions that arise is whether the university should pursue the 'sacred' or 'secular' path. In the contemporary models, the UN University in Tokyo or the North-Western University in the US pursued universalism while the Buddhist universities in Thailand have a somewhat different perspective.

The Nalanda University is being created with the avowed purpose of working towards 'building an inclusive society in a world free of war, terror, violence and fear', and creating a unique partnership between scholars and interested persons in 'understanding Buddha's teaching in a contemporary context without excluding any other form of practice from any other part of the world'. It would also seek to address what President Kalam considers the contemporary challenges of poverty: underdevelopment, environment, ecological management and endemic shortage of water and energy.

The university will also reposition Bihar in Asia, helping build a new Brand Bihar that will harness the goodwill generated by this project.

The challenge, however, lies in the nitty-gritty: financing the university, attracting and retaining researchers of repute, and so forth.

26 November 2006

Bihar: Poverty and Potential

Hopefully, the aftermath of the ongoing electoral rhetoric in Bihar will yield stable electoral outcomes. Bihar's development imperatives need de-politicization and concerted measures to reverse its serious economic decline. Here, I will focus on the current economic status and steps for quick redressal.

The word 'Bihar' conjures an image of poverty, backwardness, violence and failed governance. Media coverage of the state too seems to expect the worst: more corruption, more violence at the polls, more poverty and so on.

What are the realities behind this perception? Bihar is poor. It is very poor. It has weak infrastructure, low literacy rates and a large population.

Regional disparities in India are always worrying and the gap between Bihar and other parts of India has fluctuated over recent history. The divergence increased as other states' growth surged in the 1990s, but has recently narrowed. Bihar's annual growth rate was 5.2 per cent compared to the all-India growth rate of 5.6 per cent in the 1980s which declined to 3.46 per cent in contrast to the national growth rate of over 6 per cent in the 1990s and has recently increased. The Central Statistical Organization (CSO) figures place its average growth rate from 1993–94 to 2003–04 at 5.8 per cent per annum, just under India's 5.9 per cent per annum.

Differences in the growth of per capita SDP are however more pronounced. Bihar's per capita growth rate actually fell from 2.97

per cent annual in the 1980s to 1.86 per cent in the 1990s while for India it rose from 3.36 per cent to 4.07 per cent. Bihar's population growth rate actually increased between the 1980s and 1990s, from 2.14per cent to 2.43 per cent, while India's population growth rate declined from 2.44 per cent to 1.94 per cent.

Bihar showed only a marginal decline in poverty over this period, but not as much as the rest of India. During 1977–78 to 1983, the poverty ratio for India fell to 44.48 per cent, Bihar's stood at 62.22 per cent. Planning Commission estimates show that the poverty ratio fell from 35.97per cent to 26.91per cent for India over 1993–2001; Bihar reduced its poverty level from 54.96 per cent to 42.6 per cent. Thus poverty levels are nearly 75 per cent higher than the all-India average.

The summary poverty statistics however hide outcome variations. Bihar's infant mortality, for example, was below the national average during this period: fewer children died, proportionally. The Indian economy witnessed rapid economic growth with a very marginal decrease of infant mortality rate from 77 to 71 per 1000 births during 1991–2001, but Bihar's infant mortality rate dropped from 75 to 67 per 1000 births in this period. Similarly, life expectancy at birth during 2001 for Bihar was 65.23, higher than the national average of 64.77. But Bihar, while poor, is more equal (as indicated by a lower Gini coefficient) than India as a whole, especially in rural areas. Rural inequality in Bihar during 1983 was 0.272, below the national average of 0.291. It decreased to 0.236, while the national average was 0.266 during 1993-94, and remained below the national average (at 0.225) even in the more recent period. This is one indicator that rural growth could do much to reduce poverty.

Urban inequality in Bihar, however, started rising after 1993–94. The Gini coefficient increased from 0.283 in 1983 (compared to the all-India 0.293), to 0.324 (all-India 0.327) in 1993, and 3.41 (all-India 0.327) in 1999–2000. The recent upswing is worrisome.

Bihar is performing less well in terms of its literacy rate. During 2001, the literacy rate in Bihar was only 48 per cent, far below the national average of 65per cent. Bihar also performed poorly in the earlier period with just 32.3 per cent in 1981 moving up to 38.54 per cent in 1991. The Human Development Index, a composite of literacy, life expectancy and per capita income, has increased for Bihar like the rest of India, but Bihar still lags behind at 3.67 compared to the Indian average of 4.7.

Bihar ranks eleventh out of the fifteen major states in terms of social and economic infrastructure. Within this summary ranking, however, conditions vary. Bihar's road density, at 101.8 km per one lakh population, is higher than the national average of 25.82, in part because exploitation of the rich mineral resources required connectivity to market centres. Bihar's road network remained the same as population grew, however, leading to a decline in density from 119.73 km per lakh in 1981 to the current figure.

Bihar's railway density is also significantly higher than the national average. It has 30.22 km per thousand square km of land area, in contrast to the Indian average of 19.08. The freight equalization policy which was introduced in 1952 and remained in vogue till 1993, however, neutralized these advantages of proximate availability of raw materials with entrepreneurs preferring industrial locations closer to markets in the west and the south.

The power infrastructure is a handicap. Per capita consumption of electricity in Bihar is only 140.8 kwh, compared to the all-India average of 354.7. The power sector's endemic weaknesses: its low plant load factor, high transmission and distribution cost, insolvency of the state electricity boards, etc., has held the state back from augmenting this figure. It also limits utilization of the plentiful groundwater availability in north Bihar.

Bihar's large population, high unemployment rate and increasing social tension arising from failure to meet development aspirations, remain a daunting challenge for policy makers that go beyond infrastructure, however, primarily to institutions and governance.

Postscript

The electoral outcome was fairly decisive. A new government of Janta Dal (U) and Bharatiya Janata Party under the leadership of Nitish Kumar assumed office in November 2005. This government is purposive and development-centric. The approach to the Eleventh Five Year Plan adopted by the Bihar cabinet projects a growth rate of

8.5 per cent over the next five years with public investments of about Rs59,000 crore and private investment of Rs107,000 crore with priority accorded to infrastructure, agriculture and human resource development.

There is a marked change in perception about Bihar and the state looks forward to purposive public–private partnership.

30 October 2005

60

Resolving Bihar: Poverty and Potential

Bihar has failed in addressing its major development imperatives. This represents both an absence of a credible developmental strategy coupled with poor governance quality.

The gap between policy and implementation is not new. Land reform is an early example. Bihar was the first state in independent India to legislate on land reform. Its implementation, including conferring tenancy rights to tillers, ownership rights to sharecroppers and implementation of land ceilings was and is disappointing. Bihar never proceeded to any meaningful implementation due to a combination of inadequate political will and the enormous clout of the rich landed class: the Bihar Abolition of Zamindari Act of 1948 was challenged in court and did not proceed. It was later replaced by the Bihar Land Reforms Act of 1950, but still faced complex legal obstacles with tardy implementation. This inaction on land reform limited the benefits of the Green Revolution. The new technologies, which brought significant changes in farm incomes and agriculture sector, did not reach Bihar and land outlays and agricultural productivity stagnated. Ironically, Bihar is one of the states that could have most substantially and sustainably benefited from the Green Revolution, given its hydrological resources.

Successive governments have failed to improve governance quality. The decline in recent years has been more perceptible. A redressal would need to concentrate on seven critical components.

First, de-politicization. Almost every activity in the state is viewed in terms of caste or communal divide; vote politics overshadows sensible economics. This needs a thaw and, at least for the next five years, a shift of focus from politics to economics. The de-politicization includes civil service reforms, including improvement in the quality of the public delivery system, security of tenure, merit-based placements and reviving the confidence of field organizations, particularly in roads and irrigation which can significantly improve both the efficiency and quality of projects.

Second, improving the overall security environment by better guarantees on the security of life and property, creating an environment which can reverse the haemorrhaging of capital and managerial outflows and improving the climate for gainful economic activity is critical.

Third, the experiment of having central agencies to implement projects as part of the compensation package for the partition of Bihar needs to be accelerated and clarified. The initial goal was to cocoon these projects from the deep-rooted malaise in institutions at the state level, but there are ambiguities regarding project implementation, operation and maintenance.

Fourth, an improvement in the fiscal parameters is critical for economic viability in the least for an effective utilization of central and centrally sponsored resources. It is ironic that while the focus of multilateral institutions like the World Bank and the Asian Development Bank is poverty alleviation, Bihar, with the highest incidence of poverty does not have a single externally aided project. Any strategy to persuade multilateral, externally aided projects would need assurance on security as well as meeting minimum performance criteria for ensuring project viability.

Fifth, the comparative advantages of Bihar's plentiful groundwater at shallow depths in north Bihar whose harnessing would improve agricultural productivity. Links with improved road and tele-density along with cold-storage chains create enormous scope for value-added agro-processing activity. South Bihar's irrigation systems need significant rejuvenation and the more drought-prone areas' imaginative water harvesting and cropping patterns suited to economical use of water.

Sixth, considering that Bihar ranks eleventh among fifteen states in the infrastructure index, improved energy availability is crucial. Augmenting capacities, improving distribution networks to roads, transmission and distribution losses, unbundling electricity boards, encouraging private investment at the distribution end, setting up joint ventures for generation systems close to the nearby coal pitheads is part of the strategy. Ensuring smoother implementation of ongoing NHAI programmes coupled with upgradation for resources available for state highways and effective utilization of funds from the Pradhan Mantri Gram Sadak Yojana needs close attention. The low tele-density reflects the enormous scope for improvement even in the short run.

Seventh, the demographics of Bihar give it some distinct advantages. Students from Bihar are successful in the more competitive environment in other parts of the country and universities abroad. The given demographic profile, if coupled with significant improvement in educational systems, has multiplier benefits. Bihar's demography can become its opportunity instead of a drag. Improved education and health quality and a better investment climate will also reverse the migration out of the state and ensure better utilization of talent from Bihar.

Finally, its low level of development and productivity, sad as it is, also represents the enormous scope for improvement even with incremental investment particularly in the social sector. Among all the aforesaid factors, restoring the security of life and property which is the basic raison d'être of any state remains the critical component. The Supreme Court judgment setting aside the constitutionality of the presidential action in dissolving the Bihar assembly has raised moral issues which will inevitably remain unresolved. The least we can do is to support the government which comes to power in a development blueprint to turn Bihar's poverty into fulfilling its potential. We need to restore dignity to Biharis and restore part of Bihar's lost glory.

6 November 2005

61

The Potential of Rajasthan

I have just returned from Jodhpur after speaking to a group of NASDAQ and New York Stock Exchange Advisory Board members. They were fully cognizant of the new India which has emerged. In fact, their wives seemed even more perceptive, looking beyond growth and economic issues. The questions they posed to me covered a whole gamut of complex issues—demography, human resource development, water, local self-government, the future of coalition politics, sustainability of the current confidence building measures with Pakistan and the importance of the nuclear agreement with the USA inter alia for energy security. What intrigued me was why they had selected Jodhpur to be the centrepiece of their India visit. It was then with some surprise that I learnt that a few days ago the senior management of Credit Suisse was also here to celebrate their completion of 150 years. Earlier, the Li & Fung Board meeting was also held, not to speak of the Mastek Customer meet, board meetings of Mahindra & Mahindra and Birla Sun Life, to name a few. In the next few months, many more events are in the offing, like the Celloware conference and Micro Inks board meeting.

For its size, Jodhpur was obviously doing well in attracting so many events. Enticing events and managing them well has not been India's forte. Spain had hosted 18,566 meetings in 2003 whereas our responses are usually ad hoc, uncoordinated between various ministries and of course, the Centre and the states not acting in tandem. For too long, the need to have an India Events Commissioner has remained neglected. It is, therefore, creditable that in the absence of a coherent national policy, medium towns have gone ahead to grasp the new opportunities which the new India profile has to offer. So what do we learn from the Jodhpur example?

First and foremost, the importance of local leadership. Gaj Singh, the erstwhile ruler of the Marwar State, has bent his energies and considerable talent in repositioning Jodhpur not merely for tourism, both domestic and foreign, but to host successful events. His success stories keep growing and each experience has multiple lessons.

Second, states which offer security of life and property, broad cohesiveness of society and a sensitive local administration will meet with greater success. Rajasthan has been lucky in having the successive governments of Bhairon Singh Shekhawat, Ashok Gehlot and Vasundhara Raje which have preserved the rule of law and instilled a sense of security among its people. This can hardly be said of many other states. There is new hope for Bihar given Nitish Kumar's development-centric approach. Successive governments in Rajasthan have realized the centrality of these obligations and their catalytic role in the development process.

Third, high-quality infrastructure is, needless to say, as important as good governance. The significant improvement in national and state highways in Rajasthan, coupled with significant improvements in drinking water, drainage and sewerage in its six or seven major cities has certainly helped. Here again, the continuity of policies by successive governments has lent momentum to initiatives which commenced earlier. Rajasthan does not figure high on the Human Development Report on many indicators, particularly education and in reference to the girl child. Other development indicators like per capita consumption of electricity, assured access to cattle feed and drinking water during the frequent bouts of drought remain grossly inadequate. So what should be Rajasthan's priorities?

First, to bring about a significant improvement in its infrastructure, it need not set up multiple power plants but should become an efficient trader in power, buying from pithead power, efficiently using and trading in energy. The Rural Roads Programme linking village roads to upgraded state highways needs added momentum.

Second, to significantly improve its human resource performance indicators, particularly primary education, lowering dropout ratios through improved coverage, supervision of education quality and greater local accountability.

Third, to leverage its vast tourism potential, for the fact that all hotel rooms are fully booked for the current season and for the next two years suggests unexploited potential. Significant improvement in hotel rooms, including budget hotels, needs a transparent policy.

Along with tourism, attracting both national and international events has a multiplier effect on repositioning the brand, creating the possibility of replication and added employment. The need to lobby, leverage and secure improved air connectivity is also a daunting challenge which has eluded successive governments. Improving road connectivity and air linkages, as well as creating regional aviation hubs will support tourism in Rajasthan.

Finally, the need to attract investment, not merely in tourism but also in information technology, and above all, in agriculture. A strategy for sustainable agriculture development which optimizes both surface and underground water resources as well as harnessing traditional water conservation techniques will hold the key to Rajasthan's future. Rajasthan, given its proximity to Delhi and having successive enlightened chief ministers, is well positioned for a new growth trajectory.

The Economic Policy and Reforms Council created by Vasundhara Raje has made several credible recommendations on these complex issues. These need vigorous implementation to demonstrate tangible outcomes. While detractors both within her party and outside, coupled with rumour-mongering, have tried to derail development focus, it would be a pity if Raje loses either resolute will or abiding commitment since the government is not even halfway through its tenure. Only time will tell if Rajasthan can capitalize on its comparative advantages in becoming a major development hub.

62

The Economically Illiterate Populism of Manifestos

By the time this piece is published, the electoral verdict in Maharashtra will be out. Whatever the political complexion of the new government, the focus will, sooner or later, shift from government formation to governance. The promises made in the two joint election manifestoes will be staring at the new government which assumes office. Do the finances of Maharashtra enable their implementation? Also, there is growing cynicism about the value and credibility of promises made in election manifestoes. Incumbent chief ministers increasingly believe that if voted to power, they will wriggle out of promises made and if voted out of power, will be indifferent to the deluge that may follow thereafter! The principal party in opposition invariably makes even taller promises in a bid to acquire power and if successful, can blame the pathetic state of finances which, in all probability, they will inherit for resiling from electoral promises. All this makes election manifestoes increasingly meaningless. Let us for a moment examine the contents of the two joint manifestoes. The Congress–NCP have inter alia promised a 30 per cent subsidy to farmers to bring infertile land under cultivation; a plan to reclaim 30 per cent of 32 lakh hectares of infertile land; an increase of Rs 200 in the price of cotton under the Monopoly Procurement Scheme to Rs 2,700 per quintal; loans at 6 per cent for the purchase of seeds, fertilizers; free electricity for pumps up to 5HP from 1 July 2004; dues and penal interest waived to the extent of 59 per cent; the creation of one crore jobs and special financial incentives of Rs 2400 crore for Vidarbha, north Maharashtra, Marathwada, Konkan and western Maharashtra.

Similarly, the BJP–Shiv Sena in their manifesto which they describe as their Vachanama, have inter alia committed special assistance for paddy-producing farmers; free power to farmers for agricultural purposes; a complete waiver of loans taken by farmers for agricultural purposes; remunerative prices for agricultural products; cotton cultivators to receive 3 per cent of their deducted amount; a special financial package for unemployed workers till they get alternative employment; the removal of the development deficit of Vidarbha, Marathwada and Konkan; a Draupadi Annapurna scheme—providing foodgrain to poor at Rs 3 per kg and the construction of pucca roads for each village.

The costs of implementing these commitments are staggering and estimates could vary significantly depending on how they are calculated. Contrast these with the state of Maharashtra's finances. I had the privilege of coordinating the Maharashtra Development Report (MDR) which clearly brings out that the development of the state has lagged behind and its finances are in a perilous state. The growth of Gross State Domestic Product (GSDP) has fallen from 7.3 per cent in the last fifteen years to 6.8 per cent, 6.2 per cent and 5.2 per cent during the last twelve, eight and four years respectively and its ranking among the states during the period from 1993–94 to 2000–01 has also slipped sharply. Gross fiscal deficit as a percentage of State Domestic Product (SDP) deteriorated to close to 6 per cent during 1995–2000 compared to 2.8 per cent in the earlier five-year period. Maharashtra borrowed primarily to pay salaries and pensions and to compensate for fund losses in its PSUs including the electricity board.

Maharashtra also contracted a large stock of debt during the period of high interest rates which has led to a steady increase in its interest payments. Special purpose vehicles were created and many of the state PSUs raised money in the capital market on the unconditional and irrevocable guarantee of the Government of Maharashtra. The larger issue of capping state government guarantees through special purpose vehicles and parasital entities, defeating the broader objectives of limiting the borrowing programme of state governments within prudent limits, deserves the separate attention of the Planning Commission and the finance ministry. The total outstanding guarantees alone constitute 15 per cent of the SDP. The expenditure on interest payment which was Rs100 crore in 1980-81 and rose to Rs880 crore in 1990, crossed Rs7200 crore in 2002-03! The expenditure on interest payment as a percentage of revenue receipts rose from 5.4 per cent to the unsustainable level of 21 per cent in 2002–03. This is notwithstanding the warning contained in the White Paper on the state of finances of the Government of Maharashtra in 1999 which had stated that 'the proportion of productive expenditure showed a declining trend, the capacity of the government to service the mounting debt without resorting to even larger borrowing is undermined. The situation has further compounded in recent years with growing resort to borrowings through bonds floated by State-sponsored corporations but with debt servicing (including interest and payment of principal) being assumed by the State Government.'

Clearly, the state of Maharashtra's finances should be a source of anxiety to the new government. A leading merchant banker recently asked me whether there was 'any recourse'—clearly the recourse could not be the Churchgate station or the Mantralaya! Over the next two years, other states like Bihar, Jharkhand and Haryana, Tamil Nadu, Kerala, West Bengal and Assam will be going to polls. There will be fresh competitive populism in the run up to the elections. They will also be in disregard of the financial capabilities of these states

Unfortunately, electoral penalties for disregarding electoral pledges are tardy and come after a long time. In the meantime, there is a growing disconnect between electoral commitments and governance realities. Surely, it is not intended that while elections should be contested on party manifestoes, governance should be based on the common minimum programmes. The electoral rhetoric pays scant heed to the saner advice that it is better to under-promise and over-perform.

In the case of Maharashtra, one of the first tasks of the new government would be to repair the finances of the state, retire high-cost debt and work towards a sustainable debt-servicing profile. Beyond that is the larger responsibility of restoring Maharashtra's pre-eminent position for enabling the state to grow at rates of 7–8 per cent achieved earlier. These will require difficult decisions. While both Chidambaram and Montek Singh Ahluwalia can help, the state government would need to exhibit both administrative responsibility and political will to bring prosperity to Maharashtra, which, notwithstanding pockets of high affluence, has large regions mired in poverty and underdevelopment. Electoral promises hastily made cannot inspire trust and one cannot take the cynical view in believing what Lord Keynes had said that 'in the long run we are all dead'. One must be cautious in making commitments because to quote Keynes again he had said that 'I do not know which makes a man more conservative—to know nothing but the present or nothing but the past'. In this case, 'the past' will haunt 'the present' as a new government grapples with many complex challenges to convert the daunting promises into reality of the election manifesto. Maharashtra needs all our support in realizing its development potential to once again become an engine of growth for the Indian economy.

17 October 2004

63

Restructuring Centre–State Relations

Last week I wrote an essay about the recently concluded Stanford Mirror Conference in Patna. One of the papers presented at the conference was on 'Challenges facing the Indian economy' by T.N. Srinivasan. It deserves closer attention. The paper considers the important achievements of reforms as well as what he describes 'as reviving and completing the reform agenda'. Many of these cover familiar terrain like further tariff reduction, fiscal rectitude and particularly, vulnerabilities arising from contingent liabilities. He is also cautious about our new urge to imitate China in its SEZ policies. I fully agree with him that cocooning limited areas—unlike China we have too many sub-optimal-size SEZs—through costly fiscal concessions, instead of improving the overall investment climate through better governance and efficient infrastructure which will improve our ranking in the index of the ease of doing business, may not be the best way to go. An equally interesting part of his paper concerns institutional reforms, particularly issues of centre–state relations. Srinivasan argues with some conviction that 'the framers of the Indian Constitution adopted in 1950 opted for a centralized quasi-federal system.' This system worked well at a time when there were homogeneous single-party governments in almost all the states and the centre. However, the framers of the constitution could not have anticipated the subsequent emergence of heterogeneity in polity and the decline in institutions as well as changes in the economy that have eroded the rationale for unitary features and quasi-federal features of the constitution. In substance, Srinivasan has made four important proposals. First, alter the mandate of the Finance Commissions; let them also consider issues and efficiency of public sector entities which can impact (and indeed have done so) finances at the centre and the state. Second, unify all devolutions by doing away with discretionary transfers and multiple centrally sponsored schemes. Third, constitute a fiscal policy review council consisting of the prime minister, the finance minister and the chief ministers as well as experts to examine fiscal issues from an overall macro viewpoint which will enable the participative engagement of the centre and the states and also enable the states to question policies of the central government. Fourth, since planning in the conventional sense has outlived its utility while public investment has not, reconstitute the Planning Commission as a fund for public investment with both the state and the centre as its stakeholders which can borrow funds like the development bank to provide resources for long-term finance.

There is no doubt that the present mechanisms of centre–state consultations have ceased to be meaningful. The Interstate Council has not served its original objectives. The National Development Council is just a ceremonial body which is not presented with hard policy choices to be made and does not permit meaningful interaction. To create functional institutional entities is now a contextual necessity. The degree of fiscal bias in the devolution of resources in one form or the other, or selection of the location of central investments is not free from political predilections and depends on state governments and their friendliness with the coalition in power at the centre. Important decisions by the entral government which impact the states fiscally are rarely preceded by consultations with them. For instance, fiscal concessions in tax policies, both direct and indirect, or various exemptions take away a large corpus (as much as half of the collected revenues according to the 2007–08 budget) of funds which would otherwise form part of the common divisible pool to be shared with the states. The states have legitimate reasons to ask at whose expense these concessions are being given since they are being denied what would otherwise be part of their share. This is not to take away the budget-making powers of the central government but with the centre and the states as common stakeholders, a meaningful consultative mechanism between them is necessary. For instance, the extension and deepening of implicit and explicit subsidies or preferring populist schemes in current fashion which have an impact on the fiscal health of states are also decided without any consultations. If states are expected to behave in a fiscally responsible way, is it fair that the central government's own policies should remain above any discussion or reproach? Why can't the states discuss the central government's fiscal policies when the states themselves are subjected to examination by the centre?

The present structure of inherent biases, political predilections and differential criteria makes the present structure of centre–state relations an unequal one. The political appetite in coalition governments for constitutional changes may be low. Lot of things can be done within the existing framework and through administrative action to create new and more meaningful mechanisms for centre–state dialogues. But who will take the lead? The present central leadership, given the other distractions, may not show much urgency and inclination. So it is left to the states to consider, consult and act in concert to seek fair and rational redressal of the present embedded inequities. Centre–state relations need an innovative approach.

Epilogue

All great civilizations tend to be superstitious. Chinese astrology predicts that 2007, which will be the year of the boar, will bring a good business climate as well as general feelings of abundance. It will be a year of complacent contentment.

However, the year of the boar comes with a warning: the boar is prone to overindulgence.

How will India fare in the year of the boar? On the one hand, there is reason to 'feel good'. GDP growth has averaged 8 per cent over the past few years. The 2006 estimates vary, but even the World Bank expects that the growth rate will come in at just under 9 per cent for the year. Most forecasts predict only a modest slowdown over 2007 and 2008. The stock market has been surging: the Sensex is up 4,000 points since the beginning of 2006, and domestic and foreign investor interest should continue to strengthen as third-quarter results are announced after the New Year.

The year of the boar also brings the promise of widespread prosperity. India still has a long way to go—as evidenced by the recent release of NSSO data showing that a third of the rural population lives on less than Rs12 a day— but public and private initiatives are making inroads into rural India as well as economically marginal urban areas.

Ambitious public sector initiatives such as the National Rural Employment Guarantee Scheme, Bharat Nirman or the National Urban Renewal Mission clearly intend to make a difference.

On the other hand, the warning labels cannot be ignored. The boar's tendency for overindulgence is barely in check. The RBI's Report on State Finances for 2006–07 shows some improvement in states' deficits and debt reduction, but this is not uniform across states. The Sixth Pay Commission has also been constituted and will likely recommend a pay increase. Its recommendations are not technically mandatory for states, but they do appear to be politically mandatory.

The Eleventh Plan approach paper's call for more public investment rests on optimistic growth targets and contains ambiguous plans for locating the resources. The discussions about adjusting the FBRM targets or suspending them temporarily only postpone the underlying reality that India will either need to increase its tax realization, or achieve more results with the existing expenditures.

More tensions are on the horizon as rising energy import costs affect India's external balance. Net energy imports have been increasing since the mid-1980s from 5 per cent use in 1986 to over 20 per cent energy use in recent years.

India is also vulnerable to undermining its potential by wavering and vacillating in reforms—this aspect of the country seems to be stuck in the year of the boar. Its political institutions, a dense network of politicians and bureaucrats spread across three levels of government without a clear coordinating body or ethos, seem almost designed for delay.

All concurrent subjects (and many of the policies on the Union and state lists too) require the Union and the state governments, which often have different political constituencies and ideologies, to work together. Most policies fall under the purview of several ministries or independent departments—with fifty-one of them it would be hard to avoid overlap.

Within the ministries and public sector bodies, detailed procedural norms for procurement, consultation and audits shape decision making as much as the policy goals themselves. One former minister's comment on the system: 'No enemy of India could devise a system better designed to paralyse decision-making. Administration in India has degenerated into a system of endless correspondence and meetings as a substitute for action.'

To make matters worse, India has limited functional and purposive mechanisms for coordination across this array. Intergovernmental and inter-ministry coordination takes place in ad hoc meetings, committees, or bilateral negotiations. The Interstate Council meets, but irregularly, and its decisions are not binding. Inter-ministerial working groups have been created for particular subjects (such as infrastructure or power), but longer-standing institutional changes such as single window clearance, particularly in the states, have lagged.

Parliament could be a natural coordinating body (in addition to being one that makes laws) across levels of government and ministries, but it has limited resources for doing so.

Members of parliament are given allowances for housing, but not for research. Most of the research is done by the departments themselves. Many of the committees that examine bills ex ante are mostly ad hoc committees that are dissolved after the bill is dealt with. Many bills pass without comment or discussion.

The new year's policy resolutions for the year of the boar are simple to state but harder to elaborate. It is straightforward to say, 'Keep a prudent fiscal policy,' and less obvious exactly what spending plans should be reduced, or which taxes adjusted. It is easy to say, 'Streamline decision making,' but less obvious to identify which departments, offices, or levels of government should delegate their seats at the table for the sake of simpler processes.

We could recommend 'empowering parliament', but that would beg the question of why it has not exercised this prerogative to make the changes itself and in this effort become more relevant.

We must instead, resolve to untangle the underlying institutional features that preserve complacency and prevent change.